THE COMPLETE CANCER DIARIES

One Man's Journey into Darkness, Wonder, and Hope

by

Byron Leavitt

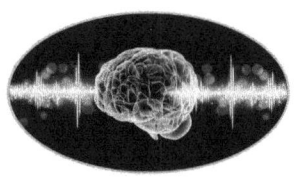

Brain Waves Press

The Complete Cancer Diaries. Copyright © 2015 by Byron Leavitt. All rights reserved.

This book may be reproduced, in whole or in part, provided all excerpts are properly attributed to the author.

In other words, feel free to share this book. Quote away to your heart's content. However, if you do, would you mind dropping me a line to let me know? You can reach me at byron@byronleavitt.com.

Unless otherwise noted, images are copyright © 2015 by Can Stock Photo (Book One as well as "Joy in the Holding," "Holy Ghost," "A Violent Love," and "Prayer Like Summer Rain") or Dollar Photo Club (remainder of Book Two). Except for the Cancer Journal and several of the Seattle Journal pictures. (Obviously.) You can reach them at http://www.canstockphoto.com or http://www.dollarphotoclub.com.

Cover art by Byron Leavitt from images by Dollar Photo Club and Byron Leavitt.

Cover and interior design by Byron Leavitt.

Unless otherwise noted, all Scripture quotations are from The ESV® Bible (The Holy Bible, English Standard Version®), copyright © 2001 by Crossway, a publishing ministry of Good News Publishers. Used by permission. All rights reserved.

Most of this content was originally published on my blog "Life Springs" at http://www.lifespringseternal.com. If you enjoy this book, go there and sign up for my email list to get more like it every week!

Inquiries can be addressed to:
Byron Leavitt
byron@byronleavitt.com

Seriously, I'd love to hear from you!

First edition October 2015. "Book One" originally published as "The Cancer Diaries," September 2014 by Brain Waves Press.

Published by Brain Waves Press. Learn more about Brain Waves at http://www.brainwavespress.com.

ISBN-13: 978-0-9907235-3-0

Table of Contents

Introduction 6

Book One

The Cancer Journal Part One	10
Wondering and Grateful	14
The Cancer Journal Part Two	17
Dare to Hope	22
Beauty in the Rain	26
Coauthoring Our Destinies	29
The Cancer Journal Part Three	33
There is Peace	39
Cross-Stitched Lives	42
This Island, Man	46
The Cancer Journal Part Four	50
Our Healer	54
Life Springs Eternal	58
Where We Go From Here	62
Until Next Time	67

Book Two

The Seattle Journal Part One	72
Joy in the Holding	76

A Violent Love	80
Behind Our Masks	84
The Seattle Journal Part Two	88
Prayer Like Summer Rain	93
Why Do You Believe That?	98
Embracing the Mystery	103
The Seattle Journal Part Three	108
In the Bleak Mid-Winter	114
I Heard the Bells	118
Advent	122
The Seattle Journal Part Four	127
Holy Ghost	132
In Our Ruins	136
The Art of Human Being	141
The Seattle Journal	144
We Are Reborn	151
Going Home	156
A Wonderful World	161
Afterword	165

Appendixes and More

10 Things to Do if You Get Cancer	170
Need Prayer?	176
Life Springs	177
What Did You Think?	177
References	178
Topical Index	184
Acknowledgments	188
About Byron	193
The Fish in Jonah's Puddle	194

This book is still for my girls and my God, who always bring me through.

And it's also for you, my friend. My hope and prayer is that, as you read this book, you will find yourself overwhelmed and overcome by the glimmering glow of wonder.

Introduction

The year 2014 was the year I almost died. It was also one of the best years of my life.

In the fall of 2013 I became very, very sick. After a false diagnosis or two and thoroughly terrifying my family at Christmas I was finally diagnosed with stage four Hodgkin's lymphoma. They rushed me into a chemo treatment plan, expecting to keep me on it for at least eight months. And four months later the cancer was completely, miraculously gone.

But this, alas, was not the story's end. Later in 2014 I had another PET scan. This scan confirmed that the cancer had, indeed, returned. It was small, but it was there. And so another chapter began: like every good sequel it was bigger, darker and more intense.

I was thrust into a new, grueling chemo regimen, but it was only the precursor to the bone marrow transplant that followed. And that's where things got really interesting.

I had nearly completed work on my book, "The Cancer Diaries," when I learned the cancer had returned. I had initially thought that book would be the end of the story, but it was only the first half. So, almost a year later, here we have "The Complete Cancer Diaries."

This book is a chronicle of just over one year of my life. It is filled with my thoughts, my musings, my trials, and my victories. It *is* about cancer, but it's also about God, eternity, life, death, meaning, forgiveness, disappointment, peace, loss, love, emptiness and transcendence. It's about never giving up, and about finding a Savior there to carry you when you have no strength left. But, perhaps most of all, it's about wonder. Wonder at a light shining in the dark. Wonder at this beautiful emerald and sapphire world we call home. Wonder at the God whose fingerprints we see stamped all over this place and ourselves.

This book is a story, but it's also divided into bite-sized chunks. Structurally it's similar to a devotional (or a diary, if you will) with most pieces representing complete thoughts as well as a part of the whole. So, if one jumps out at you, feel free to skip around. There's an index sorted by topic in the back of the book if you're interested.

I originally published many of these little ponderings on my blog, "Life Springs." And, as I did, people began to identify with the messages they presented. So I kept going, kept writing, and kept hoping that my words would inspire and support someone else. I hope that, by the time this book is done, you will be able to tell me that I succeeded.

SPOILER ALERT: After releasing "The Cancer Diaries," I received (or was made aware of) questions from several people asking if I was still alive, because they didn't want to read the book if it had a sad ending. Well, as of this writing, I'm still kicking.

Your Friend,

Byron Leavitt

Book One

The Cancer Journal
Part One

I don't know exactly when the itching began. I *do* know, however, that it started inconspicuously as some mild irritation on my calves. My wife, Sarah, thought it was an allergic reaction to body wash, so we started cycling through all sorts of different soaps to get rid of it. Strangely, nothing seemed to work. The symptoms were pretty tame and thus largely ignored for quite some time. How long I can't say: six months? A year?

In any case, the problem slowly, implacably escalated until the fall of 2013 when I finally admitted the itching was no longer "pretty tame." It spread off my calves to other parts of my body, and with each passing week grew more intense. I continued to live with it, trying to find other solutions, and slowly I became more and more miserable. In late October or early November the itching had consumed my entire body. I had hundreds of bloody open wounds ranging across just about every inch of my skin. Sleep was a fleeting thing for both Sarah and me as my incessant scratching kept both of us awake. I did develop some really awesome, creepily thick fingernails on my thumbs and pointer fingers during this period, though.

Around this same time I began to cough. I thought to start with it was just a cold, or possibly a consequence of an ear infection. But then it stayed. And stayed. And got worse. And worse.

By Thanksgiving my family finally talked me into doing something I hadn't done since I was a teenager: they convinced me to go to the doctor. And what an enlightening experience it was. We went to an urgent care clinic where I was promptly diagnosed with scabies, a highly contagious burrowing parasite similar to but nastier than head lice.

With healthy doses of skepticism and hope we took home our pesticide cream and slathered it all over my body. I still have scars from where it burned my already ravaged flesh. It was hilarious, though, watching Sarah "come down with scabies." Almost nightly she would start uncontrollably itching, which was then followed by, "Do you see this? Does it look like a spot? Or burrow marks?" Ah, the power of suggestion.

I still held out some hope, no matter how small, that the scabies medication would miraculously start working. But then I found Nebraska. Nebraska was the lump under my right arm that I discovered in the shower one day. I named it Nebraska because that was about how big it was. Okay, so in reality it felt closer to a sand dollar both in size and shape, but that's still pretty big for something that's not supposed to be there. Suddenly my hot shower felt very cold. Sure, it could be other things. But any time someone mentions a lump, the first thought that comes up is cancer. Cancer kills people. And it takes insurance or a hefty sum of money to combat it: two things I did not possess.

I also started losing weight. A *lot* of weight. Like, probably 60 pounds' worth. By the time a third of me disappeared many people started thinking there might really be something wrong with me. If only I hadn't worn that tight Christmas sweater I might have gotten away with it for a while longer.

Christmas drew closer, and as it approached my energy steadily spiraled. The cough also grew increasingly worse until I was coughing so hard and so often that it would make me throw up. A couple of weeks before Christmas I started getting night sweats, and then the week before Christmas I started getting fevers. I would get two to three a day. I didn't completely mind the fevers, though, because when I had them I didn't itch and I didn't cough. I just slept. Who knew a fever could offer such relief?

The Monday before Christmas Eve I was dealing with a fever, and did something I had done possibly only one other time in all the years I had worked at my job: I called in sick. Or, rather, I told them I would come in as soon as I got the fever under control. My pastor and employer's wife, Pastor Joel, who also happens to be a registered nurse, called me back to find out what was going on. After talking with me for a few minutes, she convinced me to go to the ER. So the day before Christmas Eve we trekked into the emergency room. They thought Nebraska was a fatty tumor and that the itching probably wasn't a big deal. They gave me a cough medicine that didn't work, took a CT scan they didn't see anything on, and sent me on my way.

But then the ER doctor left me a message on Christmas Eve and told me to call her right away. Morning or night, holiday or not. I didn't get the message until midway through Christmas, and by then I figured what's one more day? The news would be the same regardless of a few hours.

The next day I talked to the doctor. She told me that she in fact had not received the actual report from the CT scan until after I had been discharged, and that the full diagnostic was really rather engrossing. She was forwarding me over to one of their cancer doctors, because this definitely looked like an advanced form of lymphoma.

Wondering and Grateful

As 2013 slips farther behind us and 2014 is bursting out all over our madcap lives, I find myself overcome by and beside myself with an overwhelming sense of gratitude. Not just thankfulness: I believe that thankfulness is what we feel when we're given a really good movie or a cutting-edge gadget. Gratefulness is what we feel when we wouldn't have made the house payment this month without that person's help. Gratefulness is when our child steps in front of a moving vehicle and some unknown hero shoves her out of harm's way. These are maybe extreme examples, but I think they illustrate my point: thankfulness comes more from the lips. Gratefulness comes more from the gut.

Why have I felt this gratefulness so intensely? Part of it is because I have been dealing with health issues these past few months. For some reason these problems have not sent me spiraling into a whining, "woe-is-me" state, but really just the opposite: everything has a fresh significance to it. A new importance and vitality. I find my emotions towards things that are beautiful, wondrous and sacrificial to have been heightened exponentially. And perhaps that has led me to my other thoughts.

I've been thinking about the king of the world who was

born an illegitimate child to an unmarried mother. Even though he was embraced by his mother's fiancé, there was never really a question as to whether he was his or not. During a time when adultery (as this would have been seen) was punishable by stoning, he had been ruled unwanted and unworthy of life. If the voices of society had their way, he would have been conveniently disposed of. He was born not in a hospital or even a house, but in a cave surrounded by animal dung and wet straw. He was ushered into a family not of privilege, but of poverty and enslavement. He was hunted. He was oppressed. He was not the sort of person that people wrote limitless volumes of literature or grand epics about like the Greek heroes: in the world's eyes he was destined to be forgotten. But he was and is the King of the world.

I've been thinking about a man, solitary and alone, who was abandoned by every friend he had and executed cruelly — not because he had to be, but because he knew that there was no one else in the entire world who could stand in his place. I've been thinking about a man who saw his brothers drowning in the mire, and dove in with them — not just to be able to commiserate with their suffering, but to pull them up out of it and show them a better way.

I've been thinking about Perfect Love dying for his beloved.

Every day we are looking for a superhero. Someone who will be bigger than us, stronger than us, and do the things that we cannot. The superhero is not a myth. He is real. He is a champion for all people: for the unborn and unwanted, because he himself was unborn and unwanted. For the poor and oppressed, because he was as well. For the broken, sick and lost, because he was the healer and the light in the darkness. For the low in spirit, because he could lift them up. For the thirsty and hungry, because he offered food and drink that were worth far more than a meal. For the distressed and the dying, because he would go to the ends of the earth and beyond to save them. He would even conquer death to give them the chance of new life.

The superhero exists. Believe it. He is called Messiah, Christ, Hero. He is called Jesus of Nazareth.

I am broken. I am empty and I am sick. But in that desperate state I find myself saved by a superhero who is willing to cross Heaven and earth to find me, to sacrifice his life for mine, and to rise again, brilliant and regal, as the King of Creation. And beyond all of that, He is willing to lift me up out of the mire and give me a home in His Kingdom of gold. I tremble in wonder, awe and incredible gratefulness before Him. And I know He will do the same for you. In fact, he already has. All you have to do is believe it.

In recent weeks I've found myself weeping uncontrollably. It has overtaken me at strange times and in inconvenient places. But I weep because greater love has no man than this, that he would lay down his life for his friend. The God of the universe considered me worth enough to be called His friend, and to die so I might live. And for this I am immeasurably grateful.

The Cancer Journal
Part Two

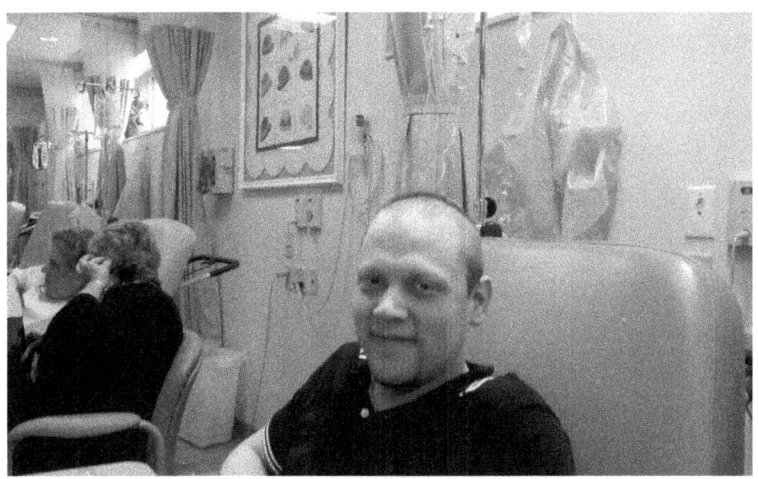

Did I mention that Sarah broke her toe?

It was late Christmas night. I was lying on the couch fighting a fever, trying to convince Sarah to go to sleep. She assured me that she would get back up if she heard me coughing, and I told her that I would be just fine. Finally she begrudgingly headed off to bed, and I fell asleep. An hour or two later, though, I started coughing.

"I'm coming, Byron!" Sarah cried. Lunging out from under

the covers, she raced through our bedroom, skidded around the corner, and –

Thud.

Her eyes grew wide. And then she screamed.

Whether she had run into the door jamb or the refrigerator is irrelevant. In either case she had felt bones move that weren't supposed to.

"I'm okay! I'm okay!" she said as I stumbled over to help her. "No I'm not! No I'm not!" she retorted as we moved her to a chair.

Several weeks (yes, that's right: weeks) later she finally went in for x-rays at her chiropractor's. He looked at the images and chuckled in that way people do while watching a hilarious video where the star probably just broke his hip. "This is awesome!" he proclaimed. "I mean, I am so sorry. But this is awesome!"

And so we entered January.

We got insurance as soon as it was available for ludicrously cheap and allowed pre-existing conditions (thanks, Obamacare!) then met with Dr. Jorges Chaves, the cancer doctor, and his nurse practitioner, Amy Lynes. Dr. Chaves was very quiet, sweet, and restrained. Amy was just the opposite: a wise-cracking bundle of energy. We thoroughly liked them both. Dr. Chaves ordered a bevy of tests, and we set out to accomplish them all. The most memorable one was definitely the bone marrow biopsy. If you have never had the pleasure of undergoing a bone marrow biopsy, let me assure you it is the most unique pain I have ever encountered. I actually felt the vial's worth of bone and goo leave my body, and it did *not* want to go.

When all was said and done we met up with Dr. Chaves again. The skin and bone biopsies had come back blessedly negative. However, the PET scan was a very different matter. My chest and abdominal cavity blazed like a radiant angel from the pit of hell. There was also a node growing on one of my lungs, and there were a lot of warning signs coming from my spleen. Basically my torso had become cancer party zone, and all their friends were invited. Dr. Chaves then said the words that are as close to a punch in the gut as words can get: I had stage four Hodgkin's Lymphoma.

There were positives and negatives to this. First of all, it was about as common as cancers get. It was also aggressive, which was ironically a good thing. My youth was another positive. On the other hand, for a variety of reasons I was classified as high risk. The cancer was very advanced. It was aggressive, which was also a bad thing. And my youth was furthermore a negative. Dr. Chaves, in his most gentle and optimistic way, said that statistically we had about a 50% chance of beating the cancer into remission.

That drive back from the doctor was one of the darkest moments of Sarah's and my lives. We had known it was bad, but now the weight of the words "stage four" pressed down on us like anvils. Pastor Joel accompanied us to that appointment, and on the drive back she asked us what we were thinking; what we were most afraid of. For the first time it hit me that I might not get to see my daughters grow up. That it was possible I wouldn't be there for my wife and girls. I'm normally good about fighting off thoughts like that, but on this trip I couldn't escape this particularly monstrous "What if?"

Sarah wanted us to get a second opinion, so we slogged through the traffic up to Seattle. The doctor was very nice, but we realized just how positive a person Dr. Chaves was. The Seattle doc, Doctor Smith, thought the chances of us killing the cancer were extremely slim, and lobbied that we take an extremely dangerous, highly damaging treatment called Baycop. It was all the rage in Germany, but in the US it was seen as so vicious that its use was practically unheard of. I was one of three people that he had recommended take the treatment in seven years. It would hospitalize me, decimate my bone marrow, make me sterile, destroy my immune system, and do potentially permanent damage to my heart and lungs, but it would definitely wipe out the cancer. We decided to take the treatment that only *might* do all these things, rather than the one that certainly would.

As we moved out of January and started treatment, I came to a number of conclusions. First of all, most people have no idea how to talk to individuals with diseases or health problems. We don't know how to handle sickness and infirmity. I can't count how many people would come up to Invalid Byron, brace themselves in some way, and, in hushed tones, whisper, "How are you *doing*?" Second, I realized that, no matter how difficult it is for you to accept it, sometimes you won't survive without the help of others. We probably wouldn't have, especially without some who went above and beyond like Sarah's mom, Pam, and my aunt, Julie. Third, I learned that sometimes our plans unfold in funny ways. I had felt for years like big things were going to happen when I hit thirty, and that it would really be the year that launched me into writing and doing what God had purposed for me to do. But instead I was going into the year flat on my back with stage four cancer.

But most of all I came to the conclusion that I was going to come through this, and I was going to bring other people with me. I was not going to just get out by the skin of my teeth: I was going to use this for God and His Kingdom. And if, in the end, I was able to touch just one life, then by God it would all be worth it.

I truly believe that it was this last conclusion that opened the door for all of the miracles that followed. And follow they did.

Dare to Hope

Do you feel it pulsing just beneath the surface? The panic, the anxiety, the sense that everything is wrong and you don't know how to fix it? The growing, suffocating, crushing weight? Sure, it can be covered up with cheerfulness, laughter and the obligatory "I'm doing just fine, thanks." But that only masks the problem. It's still simmering, waiting to bubble up and clench your heart in its icy grip. You know it's there. And you have no idea what to do about it.

I recently ordered a license plate frame for my car. The message on it states "There is hope for you. Don't give up." Not real flashy, not overly spiritual, but for me this message triggers something deep and primal. I think this is because, for so many of us, hope is a very small thing: it feels intangible, distant and almost ethereal when compared to the very present issues piling up all around us.

The problems could be something as small as an overloaded week or as large as not knowing how you're going to make your house payment. It could be a battle against thoughts you know aren't true, or it could be wondering if you're heading for divorce. It could be a cold. Or it could be cancer. It doesn't matter: they can all overwhelm and overcome us. In the real world, how can such a frail thing as hope survive against such adversaries?

But perhaps hope is more than our fears have made it out to be. Or maybe it's really just a matter of where the hope comes from.

We live in a materialistic culture that prizes what we can see and feel and experience. I mean this in the sense of the "materialism" worldview, i.e. the belief system that acknowledges only things that we can interact with, that are here in front of us, that we can measure and touch. Now, chances are most of the people reading this espouse that there are things beyond this material realm, but no matter your beliefs I guarantee that if you live in the Western world you have been affected by the mindset of materialism.

When you're sick you rely on the doctor. To do something better you rely on the newest technology. When you're feeling down you go to the mall or watch a movie or take to social networks to air your frustrations. It's all around us all the time, and it's an intimate part of our lives. We are, after all, material beings.

But what about when those things fail? What about when physical things, even people, are no longer enough? What about when life breaks and starts falling to pieces? Then we start losing trust. We start losing faith. And we start losing hope. Not only in the material world we live in, but in the God who we assume has left us to our own devices.

But the thing is, God never left us. He was there all along. We were just too busy to notice.

Job had lost everything. His wealth had been destroyed. His children were dead. His wife had, for all intents and purposes, left him. His body was sick and festering. His friends were accusing him of being a liar and a fraud. He didn't understand why this had happened to him, and he was delirious with grief. The general consensus was that God had done this to him, and that God had abandoned him. But even then Job said, "Though he slay me, I will hope in him."[1]

Even in his deepest bitterness and despair Job believed that God would show Himself strong on his behalf. But what happened to Job and his hope in the end? He audibly conversed with God. His battered, beaten frame grazed the unfathomable. Lastly, everything that he had lost was replaced, and more besides. And Job's twilight years outshone his dawn.

Last Fall I found Nebraska, like I mentioned previously. As Nebraska joined the other maladies plaguing my body I felt my world shuddering beneath me. The malignant little symptoms built one on top of the other, growing steadily heavier, and I felt myself beginning to buckle under the weight.

Despair lurked behind my eyes, in my skull and in my chest. It pressed on me, pulled me down and tried to smother me. But I never lost hope in my God, my Healer. And He has met me where I am. I am not through yet, but since beginning chemo therapy my only side effect has been fatigue. All of my previous problems have evaporated, and I have not undergone any of the trials that I am supposed to during chemo. When asked what is going on I can only point to God because what I have been experiencing doesn't make any natural sense. And God has used this time to touch lives — lives that I would never have reached otherwise. He has answered my hope. And He will answer yours.

May I exhort you with something? Dare to hope. Dare to believe against all materialistic reason in a God who still works in the world today. Dare to have faith in a man who died over 2,000 years ago and then rose again to live forever. Dare to trust in someone who we can't see or touch, but can still feel. It is not too late for you. It is not too late for your family. No matter how dark your world looks, He can shine His light and banish your nightmare. No matter how hopeless life appears, He can restore your dreams and make all things new. No matter how big your problems, hope can be bigger if it's in the right Person.

"Some trust in chariots and some in horses, but we trust in the name of the Lord our God. They collapse and fall, but we rise and stand upright."[2]

There is Hope for you. Don't give up.

Beauty in the Rain

Oftentimes when it begins to rain I will decide it is time to go for a walk. I will put on my coat and my hat, and as everyone else flees indoors I will step out into the downpour and tumult to begin the trek down our long gravel driveway. I smell the freshly cleaned air. I hear the rain colliding with the leaves, the branches, the road. And I feel the beauty of something greater than me. I find myself filling with awe, consumed by wonder. I become aware of the Father's hand wrapping around me, guiding me, guarding me. As I turn the corner I sense the whisper of God in my ear, understand the two-way nature of prayer. And I realize that everyone else ran inside to get away from this.

Don't get me wrong: I know that the rain is wet and cold and at times even oppressive. I understand why people would want to avoid it. I even do myself sometimes. But I also think that by not stepping out into the rain, by not taking that chance of getting wet, we sometimes miss out on the beauty that is as fresh as a glistering raindrop on a flower.

How often have we not seen the very best in our lives because we've been afraid to go out in the rain? How often do we, in an effort to avoid the uncomfortable, forsake the very thing God intended to use to unleash His glory?

Of course, a lot of the time we have no choice about whether we are going out into the dark, the storm, the unknown. Many times there are just no other options. Even still, how we deal with our tempest from the outset can determine where our journey will ultimately end up.

When we're in that darkness and that cold, are we looking for the little glimmers of glory? When that proposition stares us in the face and it scares us to death, are we nonetheless strong enough to embrace it anyway?

Hananiah, Mishael and Azariah (better known by their slave names Shadrach, Meshach and Abednego) were stabbed in the back by the jealous wizards and philosophers who attended with them in the king's court. Soon the king offered them a choice: they could bow and worship the golden image he had set before them, or they could be burned alive in a furnace of unimaginable fury. The three young men, however, did not waver. With steely eyes they looked their king in the face and as one voice declared:

"Our God whom we serve is able to deliver us from the burning fiery furnace, and he will deliver us out of your hand, O king. But if not, be it known to you, O king, that we will not serve your gods or worship the golden image that you have set up." The king raged and ordered them thrown into the inferno. Hananiah, Mishael and Azariah were bound hand and foot, and then they were tossed into the blazing furnace.

With a self-satisfied smirk the king peered down at his handiwork. But then he gasped. "Did we not cast three men bound into the fire?" he asked. "But I see four men unbound, walking in the midst of the fire, and they are not hurt; and the appearance of the fourth is like a son of the gods!"[3]

Their dark night of the soul came with fire. What did yours come with? And, more importantly, how will you choose to answer it?

We were never promised "the good life," pain-free and divorced from suffering. Just the opposite, in fact: we were promised trials and tribulations. But the question then becomes, what are we going to do about those things? Will we run from them, hide our faces and bemoan our fate? Or will we choose to see the beauty glimmering all around us? Hananiah, Mishael and Azariah changed a nation with their resolve, and in so doing they also met a man who was "like a son of the gods." Who knows: maybe you will, too.[4]

Coauthoring Our Destinies

How much input do we have over our own destinies?

Or, rather, how integral a part do we play in determining our little segment of the cosmic story?

One man feels like he is called by God to change a nation. So he goes and, with God's help, he does it. Did he have a choice in following the call? Or was he always destined for greatness?

Another man leaves his wife and baby and hops on a train with no destination in mind. A third one gets in a fight and ends up running from the cops. Did they take paths they were scripted to run down? Or did they have a hand in writing these dramas for themselves?

When Abraham talked to God and implored Him to save Sodom and Gomorrah if he found but ten righteous people, had God already decided that He would give Abraham what he wanted? Did He already know He wouldn't find ten, so it wouldn't hurt to promise? Or did Abraham change God's mind?[5]

Why was God horrified to find that Cain had killed Abel?[6] Why would He give nations the chance to repent if there was no chance they would?[7]

How much control do we have over our lives? Any? Some? All?

Maybe this all sounds a little too lofty and academic. But try these phrases on for size: "Everything happens for a reason." "It's all part of God's plan." "Why did God allow this?"

How many times have you heard someone say one of those phrases? How many times have you said them yourself? I'm not necessarily here to prove them wrong (though I'm definitely not here to prove them right), but I want you to see that this isn't just a dusty academic issue. This is something that affects us all. And it distinctly affects how we see God.

As a writer, I have always been very attracted to the idea of God as the Author and Finisher of our faith. It is very easy for me to see God as the great creator; the consummate, ultimate storyteller. I think that there is great truth in this: looking back at my life, I can see the plot lines winding and weaving and intersecting. I can see how this led to this which led to this, and that I would not be the person I am today if any of these things had been different. That includes the good, and the bad.

However, I feel there is another side, too. I don't think God is only interested in being the Great Author. I don't even think He's interested in just being the main character (for more on this, see Jesus.) I think he wants to be a collaborator. And I think He wants His fellow collaborator to be you.

For millions of years God spun out his story, his drama, his artistic and creative masterpiece called the universe. He spoke and light, matter and energy exploded into existence. He forged a breathtaking panoply of particles and lit the dark with supernovae and swirled clouds of dust into planets. It was mind-numbingly stunning. But it was all in preparation for what was to come. Up until that point He had written the story by Himself. But now He had formed a stage and the raw materials necessary for the coauthors to emerge, and to join in the creating.

And we did. Each one of us was given a few years (barely a flicker in the cosmic history) to write our own tales. And then our part would be done, and another would take our place. We could help to shape the Great Story, for good or ill, as we saw fit. God would maintain overall creative control, of course, but He was also incredibly generous with His narrative.

Sometimes we did the right thing, and the symphony achieved a rousing high note. Often we did not, and the chronicles plunged into darkness and depths of despair. Quite often we even crafted in shades of horror.

But here's the crux of it: I believe that we have license to shape the story. I believe that our destinies remain unfulfilled not because God didn't really *mean* for greatness to happen to us, but because we never did anything about it. We are so busy waiting for God to write something interesting, when He's really saying, "This is *your* piece. *You* write it."

I know a man who loves God. And every time I talk to him, he is anxiously looking forward to the day when God finally tells him how to apply his talents and make a difference for the Kingdom. He's not a spring chicken any more. But any day now, he's pretty sure God is going to tell him what to do and where to go. And when that day comes, boy will it be great to know what God intends for him.

What if he reaches the end of his life and God never tells him what to do? Or what if God did, and he just never listened? What if God was telling him to write his own story?

I don't claim that this is an exhaustive answer, or even a particularly good one. It's just something I've been thinking about, and I am certainly open to greater knowledge and new ideas. But for now, I would love for you to think on this: if God gave you the outline and you're filling in the details, what bits would you want to see in your life? At the end of your days what would make you feel like you made a difference and changed the world? What would send ripples through future storytellers for generations to come?

Go. Write that.

The Cancer Journal
Part Three

We went into treatment. Prior to starting, though, we were told the laundry list of side effects. These included, but were not limited to:

- Nerve Damage
- Heart Damage
- Lung Damage
- Severe Fatigue

- Demolished White Blood Cell Counts
- Demolished Red Blood Cell Counts
- Trashed Immune System
- Nausea
- Vomiting
- Diarrhea
- Constipation
- Loss of Appetite
- Acid Indigestion
- Hair Loss
- Fevers
- Mouth Sores
- Unpleasant Metallic Taste in Mouth

Now, these were not necessarily possible side effects: I was guaranteed to have two- to three-quarters of these.

The first couple treatments passed, and I was still doing pretty well. But it didn't stay that way. Around the third or fourth treatment I was hit by excruciating acid indigestion. It was so bad that I could barely function. It raged inside my guts, ripping apart my insides. The one tiny acid indigestion pill they had prescribed I take daily wasn't touching it. We talked to Dr. Chaves, and he advised me to start taking two of them a day. If that didn't work, we'd look at something stronger.

The next day I was in prayer around noon at work/church. The thought occurred to me that just because everyone else had to go through this stuff didn't mean *I* did. So I prayed against the acid indigestion and thanked God for taking it away. Immediately I felt it fading. And then I didn't feel anything. Furthermore, though there was a little bit that would flare up now and again over the coming months, that intense acid never came back. In fact, I reached the point where I pretty much stopped taking the acid pill altogether (though I would take it for a few days whenever I was chided by medical professionals.)

A similar thing happened with my blood counts and immune system. I was anemic when I went into treatment, so I was already off to a bad start. The threat of infusions was very real and often present. However, when I would get the panicked phone call telling me my counts had been flushed down the toilet, people would pray for me and the next time they would always have made a valiant rebound.

The best part, though, was the lives we touched. We soon learned that our favorite nurse, Debbie, was not only a Christian but that she attended the church renting from my church. When she learned who I was her eyes got really big and she exclaimed, "Oh! You're the one we've been making meals and praying for!" Small world, huh?

We further made friendships with Deb (no relation to Debbie,) Rita, and a number of the other chemo patients. We had opportunities to pray for many of them and talk about God. Sarah actually did far more than me in these regards, as we quickly learned that intravenous Benadryl knocks me out faster than a skillet to the skull. Because of this, I ended up sleeping through good chunks of my treatments.

As we continued on, too, a funny thing happened. Or, rather, didn't happen. My major symptoms I had going into chemo (the coughing, the itching, etc.) faded to nothing after the first few weeks. And all of the other side effects I'd been promised never manifested (with the exception of fatigue.)

I had been told that I would want to stop eating. But on the contrary, I started eating more. I was guaranteed to get this weird flavor that would flood my mouth and change the taste of food no later than the third or fourth treatment. That also failed to happen. Sure, I got a faint metallic taste in my mouth near the tale-end, but it was so minor that I didn't even tell Sarah until it was all over. In fact, there were some weeks where the taste became sweet. And the vomiting, nausea, diarrhea, constipation, et al? They didn't show up, either.

I did begin losing my hair en masse, which led to one really entertaining bath (complete with heart-warming "Eeew! What have you done to my tub?" from my wife.) Following this we decided to just shave my head. But then another curious event occurred: my hair started growing again as soon as we cut it off. This happened two more times, though each time there was less hair that fell out. My eyebrows were not so lucky, unfortunately. There were two or three robust, courageous hairs who stuck in there, but that was about it.

After a while I learned how expensive my medication was, so I stopped taking it (excepting the acid pill whenever I was told I'd get an ulcer otherwise.) This added to the conversations I would have at every doctor appointment, which I memorized:

They would say, "How are you?"

I would say, "Doing great."

They would say, "What new side effects do you have?"

I would reply, "None."

They would say, "Any nausea, diarrhea or constipation?"

I would say, "Nope."

They would counter, "Are you sure?"

"Yep."

"Any tingling in your fingers or toes?" (A sign of nerve damage.)

"No."

"What medications do you need refilled?"

"None."

"Really? Why?"

"Because I haven't needed to take any of them."

"What do you mean?"

"I haven't had any side effects."

I came to love it when people would approach me to talk to Invalid Byron. When they would start into how sorry they were for me or talking in the hushed tones, I would reply with "Actually, I'm doing pretty great. God's really blessing." It was wonderful to see the conversation immediately flip around. The person contacted me lamenting: the person left glorifying God and filled with hope.

Finally I started asking people who wanted to pray with me if they would instead pray that we would have the opportunity to change other's lives. It seems whenever I got someone to pray this we had incredible encounters the following week.

Treatments continued to roll past, and we approached the four-month mark where we would take a new PET scan and reassess the situation. I went in for the scan, and when it was over I tried to thank the technician. He had done my original PET scan, and he remembered me from the previous visit (he also remembered that I worked in a church, interestingly enough.) This was why it was strange that he didn't acknowledge me at all as I was leaving. He just kept looking at my scans with a scowl on his face. I felt a creeping dread enter me. *What was he seeing on my scans?*

There is Peace

The little boat flailed as thunder cracked the skies and lightning lit the clouds. The waves thrashed and writhed like children on a temper tantrum as panic crawled down the crewmen's throats and gripped their guts. Turning to their leader, the bedraggled sailors cried out, "Master, Master, we are perishing!"

Why did they have to yell at him so? Wasn't it obvious what was happening? Apparently not, because their master was in the back of the boat asleep.[8]

It can be very easy to assume God is asleep, or away on vacation. This is one of the ideas raised in the book "The Sunflower" by Simon Wiesenthal, a true story from Nazi-controlled Poland about the limits of forgiveness and the lives of Jews in concentration camps.[9] Life was so hellish for the people of the camps that several of them began to champion the position that God was on leave. The question – has God abandoned us – hangs heavy and unanswered in the air, a pendulous weight on the book's pages. It, along with the other questions the book more prominently asks about forgiveness and love in the most evil of circumstances, haunts you long after you have finished the book (which I highly recommend you read.)

So is and was it true? Was God absent? Does the Master not care?

One of only two characters who can be said to keep his faith in "The Sunflower" is also the only Christian. Why did he keep his faith when the Jews almost unanimously lost it? Perhaps it is partly because the Christian faith has a critical leg up on its Jewish forebear in that every time we read the gospels we see where God is amidst suffering: nailed to a cross, bruised, beaten and bloody. He isn't somewhere far off when we suffer; he is right there suffering with us.

But obviously there is a different reason Jesus was asleep while everyone else was screaming and scrabbling to life. They were consumed by fear and panic. But he was filled with something else entirely: the miracles of faith and peace. The kind that can cause a person to sleep through a tempest.

That same peace Jesus felt in the boat is available to us right now. Why? Because we have a good Daddy, and a faithful big brother who will never leave us or forsake us. They stand with us in affliction. They accompany us in the storm. And they offer us shelter from the barrage of life.

Where are you right now? Are you in the dark? Are you in the storm? Are you being buffeted by the wind and the waves and the terror that this will all end in destruction? Embrace Jesus. Ask for His peace. Tell Him where you're at and how much rope you have left. (Including if you're at the end of it.) And then take a deep breath, close your eyes, and let "the peace of God, which surpasses all understanding,"[10] consume you.

Trials come and trials go. Trust me, I know all about that. But the peace that surpasses understanding can remain. When we lean into our Creator, when we stay in that place of trust, every time fear rears its vile head we can take a deep breath, feel Jesus wrap His arms around us, and dissolve our cares in the ocean of His Care. Is it always easy? No, I won't lie and say that it is. But it's always worth it.

Cross-Stitched Lives

Just over ten years ago essentially every deep, lifelong friend I'd had walked away from me and my family. They did this because the group of churches I had grown up in told them to, and they were informed that anyone who talked to us would be tossed out along with us.

With a couple of exceptions, I haven't talked to them since.

I hadn't thought about most of them in quite some time, to be honest. But this week a dream brought them all back to my memory. I felt the hole that they had left afresh. I remembered the good, and I remembered the bad. And I started thinking about the impact each of us has on the lives of those around us.

Why do we meet the people we do, make the friends we have, lose the ones we don't any more? Is it for any particular reason? Are we all just bumping into each other at random, like blind forces of nature impacting one another? Does chance decide where we live and where we were born and who we were born to?

I don't think so. I think our moments form a deliberate pattern.

We weave in and out of each other's lives, adding to one another as we go. Some of us cross paths for only a few seconds. Others are intertwined for fifty years. In the end, though, just as we came together, we will eventually part. It is inevitable, at least in this life. But perhaps, rather than dwelling on the parting as we are so wont to do, we should instead ask what we are adding to each other while we're together.

When we are joined to another person's life are we sewing joy or tragedy? Are we building up the people we meet, or tearing them down? Do we exist only for ourselves and consequently bring pain? Or do we exist for others and bring renewal?

And when we part, what do we focus on? Do we see only the bad? The dark? The twisted little memories that perhaps drove us apart in the first place? Or do we focus on the good? Do we see how this person's life changed us, how they made us better, and strive to live for that memory?

Really, I think that most of the time it's the events that are incredibly negative in the present that most shape us into the people we are becoming. If ultimately these events strengthen us, then I think that even these things we must be thankful for – perhaps more so than the positive times. Was it hard while you were going through it? Undoubtedly. Does it still hurt to this day? Perhaps. But would you really want to go back to who you were before?

So many of us walk around in a near-constant state of brokenness, shattered by the lives that have crashed into ours. And so often it is the people closest to us who have the greatest opportunity to break us into a million pieces. Why are you holding onto that pain? What good is it doing you? Is it worth it, to live in that place of ebony emptiness? Wouldn't it be better to let the dazzling brilliance of Jesus flood that area and bring you fullness? Maybe you've even said you've forgiven the other person. But isn't it time that you said it and meant it? I am certain there were good times with that person as well, because otherwise you wouldn't have been so hurt by them. What if you remembered only those and let go of the rest?

I hold nothing against any of my old friends. In fact, what I did when I started thinking about them again was to pray for them. I hope for only the best for all of them. Some day I would be thrilled to tell them that in person.

We each are woven together for a time, and then our strands move off. But while we're together, why not work to change the other person's life for the better? Why not strive to make every life we come in contact with enriched for having met us? What can we do to change them, and consequently to change the world?

So often we're looking for our Big Purpose. For the Grand Meaning. Now, don't get me wrong, I fully believe there is a purpose meant for each of us (if we will allow it.) But maybe sometimes we're trying too hard. Maybe sometimes all we really have to do is let go of the dark, and give someone the light. Maybe we just need to make sure every thread that is stitched together with ours leaves us a little brighter.

We only have one chance to weave this magnificent mosaic called life. What do you say we make the most of it?

This Island, Man

When you can no longer interact with people according to socially acceptable norms you begin to cultivate a unique perspective on society. It can be so easy to feel like an island, even when you're surrounded by continent. You're in the throng, people are milling about all around you happy and talking and laughing, but you're still completely isolated.

You can stand amidst hundreds of others and still be utterly alone.

I've been through this recently on both sides of the aisle. On the one hand, I went for months when I had a compromised immune system, so I was forced to wear a surgical mask and this little personal air purifier that had a flashing LED on it. The air purifier drew some looks and sparked some comments, but it was much better than the alternative: the surgical mask.

Maybe in other cultures wearing surgical masks is a perfectly normal, acceptable social behavior. But in America, people look at you – and treat you – like you are currently carrying Bird Flu. This doesn't improve once they actually talk to you and learn that you have cancer. As I've mentioned before, Americans do not know how to talk to sick people. So instead they hem and haw and slink away as quickly as they gracefully can.

On the other hand, I was recently at a concert with my brother (to see the grand maestros of "Showbread" – may raw rock kill you forever and ever, amen.) As we were sitting there waiting for the show to start, a girl came up behind us and asked if the seat next to me was saved for anyone. I said it was reserved for her, she said, "Cool," and sat down next to me.

As the minutes stretched on I realized that just about everyone else was talking with friends and having a good time, but this girl was all alone. She didn't look at all like the type of person who fit in this crowd (I barely did), and I started wondering what her story was and what had brought her to this show. I started trying to come up with a way to open up a conversation with her, but I couldn't think of anything that wouldn't make me look like I was a creeper, making moves, or just weird. (I'm an introvert, all right? I realize there were all sorts of perfectly acceptable things I could have said, but for some reason at that moment nothing was coming.) Finally the concert got going and I got off the hook. But then later on the lead singer said that the only reason the band still existed after all these years was because of Jesus. Just about everyone in the crowd went crazy. Except for this girl.

Am I making too much of this? Maybe. Probably, even. But as we left that night, I couldn't help but wonder if I had missed out on an opportunity to bring a little brightness to her life. And I wondered if she had remained an island because no one had invited her to join the mainland.

Actor Robin Williams died recently of an apparent suicide. Many have said he was in the midst of a deep depression. It would seem even fame, money, and fans don't cure us of our loneliness. In fact, in Mr. Williams' case, I wonder if it made it worse; if being surrounded by so many who wanted a piece of him, criticized him and idolized him made him more alone than ever.

Which of these are you? Are you on the island looking in? Or are you on the continent glancing out? I'm going to guess it's been a bit of both.

It can be so easy to become an army of one. Don't let it happen. Don't let isolation envelope your life. You weren't meant to journey through this world alone: you were meant to influence and be influenced by others. Do people shun us or not understand us or talk behind our backs? Sure. But *we* are the ones who choose to let that burn us. *We* are the ones who decide to rise above the dirt or be buried by it. We can either overcome or be overcome: the choice is ours.

It's so easy to make our church a glowing screen and skip the human connection altogether. It's so convenient to make our social lives Facebook rather than face-to-face. I'm not saying any of these things are wrong in and of themselves, but when they become our Wilson[11] we have a serious issue.

However, we also have the flip-side of the coin. A stranger walks into your social sphere and you suddenly find yourself at a crossroad. It's so much more comfortable to carry on as you were. It's far less trying to pretend you don't see her and let her pass. And chances are there will be no skin off your back for doing just that.

But what if you are the one and only glimmer of light she will see? What if your comfort is consigning her to darkness? It's easy to brush off that thought as silly or severe. But how do you know?

What if that social misfit is in a place as dark as Mr. Williams, and a word from you could save his life? What if the wall flower just desperately needs to know she matters and that she's beautiful? What if the outcast hungers deep in his soul to be told that he finally belongs? How can we ever be salt and light if we never let anyone taste or see?

Ironically, it is incredibly easy in this connected age to find yourself that solitary island. But we were never supposed to be. You were meant for so much more.

Have you been hurt before? Burned? Cast off? Welcome to the human race. But, to paraphrase/quote Rob Bell, the question is where will we go from there? Will we be bitter or better? Closed or open? More ignorant or more aware?[12] We choose if we stay out in the cold, and we can choose if others do as well.

May we choose warmth.

The Cancer Journal
Part Four

Two days passed following the PET scan. I tried to push the technician's look out of my mind, but without much success. And so we came to Friday evening. I was driving when the doctors' office called, and because I didn't want to "break the law" I didn't answer it. Good excuse, no? If you don't want to hear bad news right away, just send them to voice mail because *you're driving!* Mad props, state patrol!

When we parked, though, I finally screwed up the courage

to listen to the message. Amy's voice came on the phone. But she didn't sound morose: instead she sounded ecstatic. She said, "Hi, Byron, this is Amy from Dr. Chaves's office. I just couldn't wait until next week to give you the good news. The PET scan looks fabulous. We can't see any cancer, anywhere… We'll go over the PET scan in detail when we see you, but there has been complete resolution of all of the hot spots… So you and the Good Lord doing all that great work, congratulations, and you guys have a fabulous weekend!"

I sat there, dumbfounded. And then I chuckled.

Sarah said, "What did she say? Play it for me!" So I replayed it on loudspeaker.

Can I tell you the strangest part of this whole evening? It was that we didn't start jumping up and down or shouting right away. Instead, we almost felt sober. Sounds weird, doesn't it? But the truth was that we'd been having such a great time and impacting so many lives that we didn't want it to end. However, I saw the hand of God all over this. And I knew from experience that we had to lean into Him and trust Him, just like we had so many times before.

I told Sarah as much. Slowly we allowed ourselves to start getting excited and to step once again into the unknown. And we started planning how to tell people. Because the thing everyone had been praying for had happened: through the help of modern medicine and the power of God, *I had been healed.*

How can I definitively say that God healed me? Good question. Here's the part that rankles me: I can't. I can only go on the evidence presented to me and infer from that the best answer. But here's the evidence, to the best of my comprehension: *no one* expected me to be over the cancer at four months. Not the doctors, not me, not the PET tech. Had it happened before? Sure. But it was *extremely* rare. Especially for high risk, stage four dudes with dangerously advanced symptoms. (Remember: I had, at best, a 50% chance of *beating* the cancer, period. I doubt the odds of it being gone at the halfway marker for treatment were anywhere *near* that.) Also, I know I had a good attitude, but how could that have possibly been enough? I further know that my body is resilient, but come on. On top of this, the fact is that we don't know when the cancer actually died. It could have been at three months. Or even two. We just don't know.

Second of all, there are all of the little miracles that happened leading up to this. From the acid indigestion miracle to the blood counts to the almost complete lack of side effects to all of the other little things that added up to be one big thing along the way.

Third, there are all of the other lives that have been impacted. I have seen at least one healing following mine that was a direct result of my testimony and people's prayers. Jim had been trying for years to get his thyroid to work properly. And is it coincidence that the week after he heard my testimony, when I specifically told him he was next, he suddenly had a normally functioning thyroid and began weaning himself off the medication he had been on for years? Not just because he suddenly felt fine, but also because his (thoroughly perplexed) doctor said to? That could stretches incredulity rather far, in my opinion. And he is just one of many who God touched through this story.

But in the end, this, like so much of life, has to be taken a little bit on faith. Having said that, when you combine the evidence I mentioned above with my faith, I can tell you that, yes, I believe God healed me of stage four Hodgkin's

Lymphoma. Was it instantaneous as so many expect a miracle to be? No. But, honestly, I wouldn't have missed out on these experiences for the world. And God's not done yet.

Throughout our treatment God used many people to bless us in a multitude of ways. But a more common way we were blessed was through financial gifts. It started coming in while we were still in chemo mode. But it *really* started coming in once we decided to trust God and start stepping *out of* chemo mode. I can now say that, through many wonderful, generous people (and one mighty little lady in particular), we are coming out of this free of medical debt — something that I never could have imagined was possible back in December. But God's not done yet.

Oh, remember previously when I mentioned that I thought my thirtieth year would be the year I started stepping out into what God had put me on this earth for? It turns out I was right. God has used this cancer, from the very first time I wrote about it, to launch me. It has touched lives that I would never have had any contact with otherwise. And it has transformed both me, my family, and many, many others. What more could I ask for than that? But God's not done yet.

This has been a little bit of my story. I hope it has blessed you, and that you'll share it to bless others. But barring that, I hope it has made you think and consider: is there more to existence than I thought there was? Does God still work today? Is there reason to wonder? *What if?* And, lastly, I pray that the battle-cry on your lips (for yourself, for your circumstance, for your family, for your region, your country and the world,) will be this:

God's not done yet.

Our Healer

I stood in the shower, tears melding with the spray from the showerhead on my cheeks. With nothing else to do, I sang the song "Healer" by Michael Guglielmucci as well as my tortured throat would allow: "I believe you're my healer. I believe you are all I need."[13] Many days it was all I could do to sing this song, or ones like it. Other days, when I had more strength, I would walk what Mark Batterson calls prayer circles around our house.[14] Both of these activities were fine, good and helpful.

But really, there is very little *I* did. All I really did was embrace a stubbornness that God and I were going to win. The hundreds or thousands of people around the world who learned about my condition did much more than me. Their prayers encompassed and blanketed the globe, and sent a sweet savor up to Heaven. I know many of us have a tendency to embrace the "If it be thy will" prayers, but I have a hard time believing that many of the people praying for me did this. I believe they went something more like this: "Father, heal him!" Why? First of all, because I know a lot of the people praying for me. But most of all because God did. In four months.

Why did I recover so miraculously when so many others didn't and don't? What made me special? Was it, as I've been told over and over again, my attitude? Was it because of the way people prayed bold prayers of faith over me? I *do* know that these were both vital factors, but I've seen people with as much faith or more than me still die from this, and I myself have prayed boldly for someone only to watch them pass away two days after.

Was it in part because of my chemo? Definitely. Or the vitamins I was taking? Probably. But *no one* was expecting me to be over this in the time it took, if I got over it at all. And how can those things explain the complete lack of side effects I experienced (apart from fatigue)? Another crazy thing? Yes, we learned at the end of four months of treatment that I was cancer-free. But it could have easily happened at three months. Or even two. My cancer-free date of 5/9/14 was just the day that we got the results of our test.

Or was it just not my time to go? Most assuredly it was not, but I've known others who went out when it arguably wasn't their time. (Don't believe that's possible? For a converse of this idea, read about Hezekiah in the Old Testament.[15])

Was it because I never gave up? Surely that was a part of it. I've seen many who gave up and only survived for a few days past that point. They were given a choice, and they took it. Who could fault them for that? However, I don't believe I was ever pushed to that point. People would often step into my office and say, "I shouldn't be complaining. Look at what you're going through." And in my head I would say, "You know, this really hasn't been that bad."

And through all this the question still persists: *why me?*

Can I be honest with you? I think that sometimes people need a rallying point. A lightning rod, if you will. They need the go-ahead to go ahead and believe that they can make it, too.

We've lived in this twilight land for so long that we don't know whether we're moving into daylight or nighttime. We *want* healing to be true. We *want* to know that God's promises are as valid today as they were thousands of years ago. But *we just don't know*. We want to know this God and trust in this God and love this God, but can we? Or should we grow jaded? Do we simply give in and call anyone who believes in this stuff a hypocrite or a misled huckster? The evidence seems to mount and mount against healing and the God who says He heals, but deep in our hearts I think we still want it to be true. I think there's a part of us that *needs* it to be true.

The question, after all, isn't just "does God heal?" The question is also, "does God love me?"

When we finally knew what we were dealing with, I determined that I was not going to come through this thing alone. What I mean is, if I could change just one life through this process, if I could show just one person how real Jesus and the Father were through my suffering, then everything else would be worth it.

Perhaps God has made me a gateway. Why not come on in and find out?

"By His wounds you have been healed."[16] Do you believe that? *Can* you believe that? You should. It happened to me. It can happen to you, too. I don't care if it's cancer or an incurable disease or an imbalance in your body or brokenness in your family. God can heal you just as easily as He healed me. Healing wasn't just for the old Apostles. It's happening today. His stripes heal just as well now as they did back at the first church.

I'm not singing the "Healer" song for me any more. I'm singing it for you. He is *our* healer. Now it's your turn.

Do you need prayer? Then, please, let me know. You can do this either on my website at lifespringseternal.com, or by email at byron@byronleavitt.com. I would love to pray with you, and if it's okay with you I'd love to get other people praying for you as well. I have a prayer page on Life Springs that's there for this very purpose.

Let's stand together with some rabid faith and really believe God's as good as His Word. And, by all means, when your healing comes, don't keep it to yourself. Tell me. Tell the world. Scream it from the rooftops.

A wildfire starts with very small sparks. Why can't those sparks be us? Let's light the fire together.

Life Springs Eternal

When was the last time that you thought about death?

Does it sound morbid to say that I think about it a lot?

Now, sure, it's probably natural for someone who's been fighting cancer to think about death somewhat. After all, for many people it is a sharp slap in the face that, contrary to popular opinion, they are probably not the exception to the rule of mortality. But this isn't a new thing for me. I have thought a great deal about death for a very long time. Sometimes it has scared me. Sometimes it has made my faith waver. Because, in the end, we all have to face the Great Dark.

Some people are healed of a deadly disease. Some receive miracles and victories and happiness. But, in the end, every miracle is temporal. Not a one of them lasts forever. Eventually everything — and everyone — turns to dust. Eventually death comes for us all.

And, if the materialist worldview is right, oblivion will swallow each of us up, and that will be our end. There are no happy endings. There is only tragedy.

A couple of years ago I was studying the Old Testament. Imagine my surprise when I discovered that the early Jews felt very similarly to the materialists. Even King David. He didn't believe in an afterlife as we do, but in Sheol: a dark shadow world where people could not truly be said to be alive.[17] His son, Solomon, one of the wisest men in history according to the Bible, said, "Who knows whether the spirit of man goes upward and the spirit of the beast goes down into the earth?"[18] Then, later, he said, "For the living know that they will die, but the dead know nothing, and they have no more reward, for the memory of them is forgotten."[19] Most early Christians did not believe in an afterlife per se, either. They believed in a resurrection of the dead, but until that happened their brothers and sisters slept a sleep only God could wake them from.[20] Even this was a highly controversial idea in first century Judaism, though, and it had squarely divided the Levites. Some of them chose to hope in the resurrection (the Pharisees), but the scriptural purists (the Sadducees) did not believe in any such thing.[21] In fact, our idea of Heaven arose mainly from a very interesting source: the Greek philosophers, more specifically Socrates and Plato.[22]

These realizations brought me to my crisis of faith: not in God, and not in Jesus, but in Heaven. In the afterlife. In the question, "Is there more?" Or were the early Jews right? Would we all, in the end, be devoured by the ravenous Nothing? By the Unending Black?

But then an idea occurred to me. Creation begins in blackness. What if, in the blackness of our oblivion, the Creator was shaping something new?

Around this time I began studying near-death experiences. These stories of people who came back captivated me. They expressed the wonder and the joy of the afterlife that I had lost.[23] I studied consciousness. I strove for a deeper understanding of Heaven.[24] And a spark ignited afresh in me that had previously guttered to embers.

What if there *is* more?

What if there's hope?

What if we desire another life – a better world – for a reason? What if we have heard rumors of eternity because the rumors are true?

Why did Jesus tell the other man on a cross, "Today you will be with me in Paradise"?[25] Was Paul talking about a near-death experience in 2 Corinthians?[26]

What if there's a light at the end of the tunnel?

As our Western culture has become mortified of death, the Christian Church has followed suit. For instance, it is taboo in much of Christian music now to sing about Heaven or what comes after, because we have sanitized our inevitable future and focused solely on the here and now. I'm not saying it's a bad thing to sing of God's everyday grace, but we are doing ourselves a disservice by not imagining the future. We are missing the end of the story. And the end is this:

Every life ends in tragedy, for every life ends in death. Darkness eats away at the vision, the chest gives one final heave and is still. All those hopes, dreams and memories, all the friends, laughter and love, are eradicated in one instant of oblivion. Mourning in a moment swallows joy whole. But then, in the midst of the tragedy, in the macabre stillness, there is a burst of light. The man once dead casts off the shell that has encased him, and rises from the ashes of his spent existence. And so it is that at the final call, the last tolling, when the villain has won, death has swallowed life and all lies dark and wasted, that the Great Author throws one final turn in the story. And suddenly the life, in a blaze of glory, rises anew. Reborn. With a new chance. A new hope. And only then is there the possibility of a happy ending.

A happy ending is really just the chance for a new beginning. Without God there is no new beginning. Without Heaven and the afterlife and the Kingdom there is no victory. And without the Lord Jesus Christ there is no example. Jesus's greatest message of hope wasn't only that he died for our sins. It was that He showed us that it was possible to rise again.

"No chilling wind or poisonous breath
Can reach that healthful shore.
Where sickness, sorrow, pain and death
Are felt and feared no more."[27]

"O death, where is your sting?"[28]

In the end, Life Springs Eternal.

Where We Go From Here

"Hope deferred makes the heart sick."[29] What a placid way to describe how the venom of disappointment poisons the soul.

Every week I ask God what He wants me to write about to help the most people. And every week I get an answer. This week the answer was "disappointment and discouragement." Sometimes I have experiences after learning the theme that help me in my writing. (This happened with "This Island, Man.") I'd already been dealing with some disappointment and discouragement, though, so I thought I had my "teaching from experience" story for the week. I was wrong.

We had a doctor's appointment Thursday to go over the results of my last PET scan, where we heard there were indications the cancer was returning. There were only a couple little spots, but that didn't change the fact there were spots. Could they still be something else? Yes. We will biopsy them to make sure, but if they are lymphoma we will be starting down the chemo road once again.

Now, I'll admit, there's a part of me that suspected something was amiss. When we had the CT scan prior to the PET scan, I had a feeling there would be something on it. Not a dread, just an impression. Same with the PET scan. So I can't say I was beside myself with shock. But disappointed? That's a whole other matter.

There's a part of me that thinks, does this mean I wasn't healed? Could I really have been that wrong?

There's a part of me that thinks, it's starting all over again.

There's a part of me, the really tired part, the part that never completely recovered from the last chemo, that's just sighing, wondering what will hit us next. Especially considering everything else I've been dealing with recently. (To protect others I won't go into the rest of my recent disappointments and discouragements. I don't want anyone to get hurt by my words or feelings.)

There's a part of me that wonders if I have misled people in what I've said, in what I've stood for. This is the one that plagues me the most.

So where do we go from here? When the rug's been pulled out from under us how do we keep moving forward?

How can we even be sure what direction *forward* is?

We start by reading this.

"Therefore, having this ministry by the mercy of God, we do not lose heart. ... For God, who said, 'Let light shine out of darkness,' has shone in our hearts to give the light of the knowledge of the glory of God in the face of Jesus Christ.

"But we have this treasure in jars of clay, to show that the surpassing power belongs to God and not to us. We are afflicted in every way, but not crushed; perplexed, but not driven to despair; persecuted, but not forsaken; struck down, but not destroyed; always carrying in the body the death of Jesus, so that the life of Jesus may also be manifested in our bodies. ...

"So we do not lose heart. Though our outer self is wasting away, our inner self is being renewed day by day. For this light momentary affliction is preparing for us an eternal weight of glory beyond all comparison, as we look not to the things that are seen but to the things that are unseen. For the things that are seen are transient, but the things that are unseen are eternal."[30]

I've been reevaluating what I know to be the purpose for my life, and my priorities. I've been taking a second look at what's happened to me the past few months. I've been working to forgive those who have hurt me. And I've been tracking down the light at the end of the tunnel. I think I've just about found it.

Can I now admit that what happened to me over these past few months had no more to do with God's healing power than any run-of-the-mill chemo therapy treatment does? That I was just lucky or resilient? No. I can't. It was just too weird. There were too many strange occurrences and uncommon coincidences. No matter what the outcome now, I cannot say with a pure conscience that I was not touched by God.

I still believe that God is our healer. Having said that, we still have biopsies to accomplish of the affected regions. I am believing that those spots will be found to be benign, or to be gone altogether. But if they're not, I am, once again, going to lean on the example of Hananiah, Mishael and Azariah: I believe that God will save me from this. But even if He doesn't, I will remain firm. God has proven Himself to me more times than I can count. Why would I forsake Him now?

If I must travel down this road again, then so be it. There must be more lives for me to touch going the one way than going the other. I will not fail. I will stand strong. And I would very much appreciate you standing with me.

There are many things that are different about this time than the last. I'm not going into it flat on my back, for one. But most importantly, I'm not afraid any more. I'm not afraid of this cancer. I'm not afraid of changes to my job or family or life. And that is, for me, a very significant difference.

Disappointment and discouragement can unravel our lives, if we let them. They can poison our souls and leave us only a husk of the person we were supposed to be. But we can choose to rise above them. We can forgive. We can embrace the change. We can fight through and blaze a new trail. We can dare, against all materialistic reason, to hope. And we *can* find the light.

Who knows: maybe, when we finally reach this new destination, we will find it to be much greater than the dream we were originally chasing. Maybe, when all is said and done, we won't see any other way it could have gone.

Until Next Time
(An Afterword)

"A happy ending is really just the chance for a new beginning."

By this definition, perhaps this is still a happy ending.

This wasn't how the book was supposed to end. In fact, it didn't end this way up until I was days away from finishing it. But, as any writer will tell you, sometimes the story surprises you in the last turn. Just like life.

I wrestled with whether to include all of the content that I did in here. I even struggled a bit on if I should release the book at all. But, in the end, I went with every bit of it. I still believe it to be true, and I still believe all of the messages to be valid. The little blazes of light were enough for me to finish this project and leave it intact. Hopefully you agree.

I don't know what the future holds. I've seen glimpses perhaps, but the coming months are still murky for me. I do not exaggerate when I say that everything in my world is now in flux, with the blessed exception of my family. I have rarely been this unmoored in my life. So why do I feel such peace?

Before I received the impression that the last essay in this book would be on disappointment I seemed to hear God say that he was opening doors that no man could close, and closing doors no man could open. I know that's part of my peace, because that happened before I knew anything was going on. But more than that, I am at peace because I have a good Daddy. My Heavenly Father has never left me. He has never forsaken me. And He's not going to start now.

Maybe you're in a similar place. Maybe the darkness is closing in all around you, and you don't know how to find the light (much less take a breath.) Don't lose hope. Don't lose heart. There is a Champion of Light fighting for you, whether you see him or not.

Why does darkness exist? Why does it so rudely invade our lives? May I put forward the idea that it exists to showcase the light? After all, we would have no idea what light even *was* if we were not first acquainted with darkness. To paraphrase the movie "Vanilla Sky," how would we know what is sweet if we didn't also know what is sour?

But though we are buffeted on every side, there is still hope. We can make it to daybreak. I truly believe that. For me *and* for you.

Thank you for reading. I hope that, somehow, this little book has touched you -- whether it's just made you think or shown you another perspective or maybe, just maybe, moved you in some deeper, more wonderful, way. Regardless, I'm grateful you've stuck with it all the way to the end.

But this brings me to a question. If this collection has impacted you, would you do me a favor? Share it with someone who needs it. Pass it on to a friend or a family member or a coworker. And then get involved online at http://www.lifespringseternal.com. Sign up for the email list. Take a look at the prayer page. Let me know what's going on with you. Let's not lose touch.

I thought The Cancer Diaries were finished, but it seems there could very well be a volume two. I look forward to sharing it with you, and all of the miracles it will surely contain, when the time is right.

I pray that you find peace, I pray that you are blessed. And I pray that every day you experience the life-giving wonder of God.

Until next time.

Your Friend,

Byron Leavitt
September, 2014

Book Two

The Seattle Journal
Part One

I was halfway through 2014 when my whole world flipped once again. I had made it through cancer. I had celebrated and trumpeted my victory. My family and I were starting the process of reconstructing our lives.

And then they found the spots.

That's where this story begins.

Summer had arrived, and with it had come a change to

our "new normal." Chemo therapy had ended. My place of work had expanded their reach, leading to a greater burden on the staff. And I was trying to jump from 50% operational to 110% overnight.

I crashed.

I couldn't do it. I felt myself stumbling more and more every day. My endurance was further eroded by my general frustration which, naturally, caused ever greater frustration. I knew I was drowning, and I felt like people in leadership were helping it along.

Projects were taken from me that weren't really mine to begin with, but that I had grown very attached to. And all the while I felt myself crumbling under the pressure.

Then the results of my most recent PET scan came back.

The spots were very small. And there were only three or four of them. But that didn't change the fact that they were there. And suddenly we were flung right back into cancer mode.

It wasn't all bad news, though. Because of the spots I got a weekend off.

Dr. Chaves, my oncologist, pounced. He was extremely alarmed by this development, particularly because the cancer had returned so quickly after being defeated. Immediately he laid out a new treatment plan: we would start with a different chemo therapy called ICE, and then we would move directly into a bone marrow transplant.

The term bone marrow transplant is slightly misleading and incredibly mystifying. What the heck even is it, how does it work, what does it do? Basically, it's where the marrow in your bones is nuked with what the doctors term "a lethal dose" of chemo, literally killing your immune system and the factory inside your body that creates blood cells. It also hopefully kills whatever cancer remains in your body. Then, when your body starts to falter, fall apart and shut down, they inject you with stem cells (either taken from your own body at some point prior – called an autologous transplant – or taken from another person – called an allogeneic transplant.) These stem cells latch into your bones and start recreating the systems that had been destroyed by the chemo.

Because of its highly toxic nature, ICE (the coolest chemo around – cue drum roll) required that one of its bags be delivered over a 24-hour period – which meant it was an in-patient procedure rather than the out-patient chemo I had always received in the past. The plan was that I would have two rounds of ICE, and then my wife, Sarah, and I would trek up to Seattle (the only place they really do transplants for lymphoma in the area) and have my stem cells extracted, as I had been deemed able to have an autologous transplant. Then we would come back down for another round of ICE, and at some point after that we would move up to Seattle for a couple of months to complete the procedure.

I chugged through the first treatment of ICE without incident, then started down the stretch toward the second. Days before my admission, though, I received a call from the Seattle Cancer Care Alliance. They exclaimed about how excited they were to have us staying with them once round two was over.

I said there must be some mistake. We were only heading up there to harvest stem cells at this point, and then we would be returning to Tacoma.

They replied that my information was incorrect. We weren't just going to collect stem cells: we were going to begin my treatment in earnest, and we would need to move up there starting on October 9th.

I had a conversation with my employers, and they informed me that they would not be able to support me financially while I was away. I told them I understood, and that God would provide for us.

A few days later I had my second round of ICE. And the following week I dropped everything at work, Sarah and I packed our suitcases, we kissed our children goodbye, and then we climbed in our black Pontiac G6 and set out for the madhouse metropolis of Seattle.

October 9th, for us, was the day everything changed.

Joy in the Holding

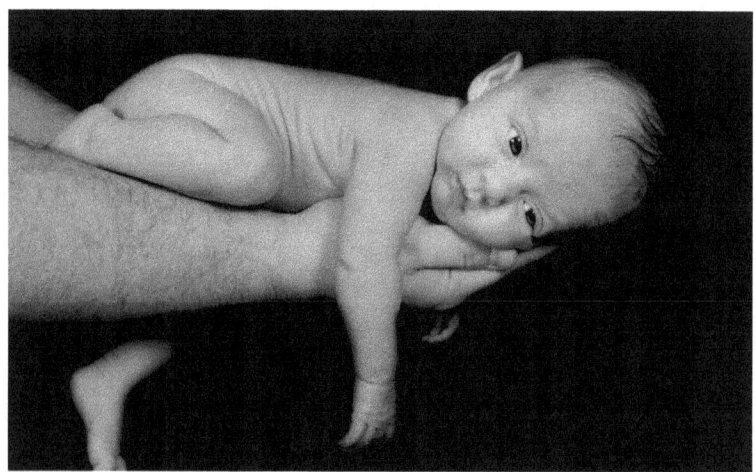

So here I am, in another chemo treatment. I've had an IV hooked up to me for several days now, and one bag of glorified poison trying to take out my bladder for the better part of 24 hours. (It hasn't succeeded.)

The doctors and nurses are once again beside themselves with my attitude, and with the general lack of side effects that have hit me. (Apart from some nausea which I prayed away in the middle of the night, there hasn't been any.)

Since we learned that the cancer was back I have had

several very seasoned, loving, mentor-types ask me if I am angry at God for letting this happen. Especially after such a miraculous recovery last time, and such a seeming triumph. I have always responded that I am not angry at God. They have then frowned and said, "Are you sure? Because it's natural to be angry at God. It's okay if you feel that way."

But I have never been angry at God (either now or, to my recollection, prior.) He gave me as much warning as anyone's ever got. And, as I pointed out before, every miracle has a shelf-life, anyway — just like us. This particular shelf-life was just a little shorter than some suspected it would be. But more than any of that, I know that God loves me. I know that Jesus has my back. And I know that, no matter where I am, no matter what I'm going through, I am being held.

I was in a conversation with a coworker recently, and she brought up a philosophy test she took (and bombed) in high school regarding if happiness was actually something that could be attained in a lasting, lifelong way, or just a fleeting emotion that was here one second and gone the next. Most of the philosophers quoted in the class said that happiness was the latter, and the former is an unattainable pipe-dream. I actually agree for the most part with the philosophers about happiness. However, I think there's a whole other dynamic to well-being, and that is joy.

For me, joy is something completely different from happiness. Happiness comes and goes. It is a flitting, inconstant emotion that jaunts where it will and allows no man to grab hold for very long. But *joy* is a choice.

You can be having the day from hell and still be filled with joy. Not so with happiness. You can choose to be ruled by your emotions, or you can choose to let joy overrule them. I always try (and often succeed) doing the latter.

But where does this joy come from? How can a person be the life of the party in a cancer ward, when that person has cancer himself?

It's because the joy doesn't come from me. It comes from Someone Else.

Psalms 16:11 says that "You make known to me the path of life; in your presence there is fullness of joy; at your right hand are pleasures forevermore."

In John, Jesus says, "These things I have spoken to you, that my joy may be in you, and that your joy may be full."[31] A little while after that, He says, "So also you have sorrow now, but I will see you again, and your hearts will rejoice, and no one will take your joy from you."[32]

In Romans Paul says, "For the kingdom of God is not a matter of eating and drinking but of righteousness and peace and joy in the Holy Spirit."[33] Later, he follows that up with, "May the God of hope fill you with all joy and peace in believing, so that by the power of the Holy Spirit you may abound in hope."[34]

And James makes a fascinating contribution to the discussion when he says, "Count it all joy, my brothers, when you meet trials of various kinds, for you know that the testing of your faith produces steadfastness. And let steadfastness have its full effect, that you may be perfect and complete, lacking in nothing."[35]

What do these verses tell us about the nature of joy? Not happiness, but the joy that comes from the Holy Spirit and God Above? They tell *me* that it is more than an emotion. That it is something that can, and should, be with us always.

And that, when trials abound, we should find it even there.

This is what I have found to be the case. This is why I am such a "happy" person. It's not because I'm happy at all. It's because I am infused with a holy joy that does not begin or end with me.

I am able to rejoice every day, because no matter what my circumstances look like, I know that I am being held in the tender, powerful hands of my Heavenly Father. I know that I am being cradled in the wings of the Almighty God. I know that my big brother Jesus is fighting for me without ceasing. And those are incredible facts to know.

When the trials of this world come to call, do they find happiness in you or joy? Would you like some more of the joy I'm talking about and a little less of the sometimes-there happy vibes? Then pray to God. Tell Him you want that joy that overflows and abounds. Tell Him that you want that fruit of the Spirit which knows no beginning or end, but somehow makes its home in your tiny vessel. (And that goes for all of the fruits of the Spirit by the way: in fact, that goes for the Spirit Himself.) And then, when the trials *do* come (or if they've already arrived), count it all joy.

A Violent Love

"For the Lord your God is a consuming fire, a jealous God."
36

How many times has this scripture, and those like it, been used to condemn God as small, petty and all-too-human? This is a favorite of atheists and skeptics the world over: jealousy is a *human* emotion, and a baser one at that. It is an emotion common in the old gods of the Greek pantheon and others. So then how is the God of the Bible any different from these old, discarded deities of the past?

"The kingdom of heaven has suffered violence, and the violent take it by force."[37] The ESV says in a footnote that this could also mean "the kingdom has been coming violently." What if there is none more violent than God? (It is His kingdom that has been coming violently, after all.) Does that scare you?

But what if God's violence is not our violence? What if His jealousy is not our jealousy? I wish to consider the idea that what we are talking about is the violent, unstoppable, uncontrollable love of God.

We are so quick to think that how God loves (a word we have cheapened to a dime's worth with phrases like "I love that movie" and "I love their cheeseburgers") is just like how we so often love - inconstantly and fickly. But His love is infinitely bigger than our understanding of it.

> We see God's love as a wistful wisp of smoke,
> Perhaps a brief inhaling of beauty and then tragically gone.
> But it is an unstoppable, intentional tornado of purpose,
> An unquenchable eternity of pure, jealous fierceness,
> Ripping asunder everything that stands between it
> And the embattled, enchained heart whom it most desires,
> The object for which God burns
> Brighter than a thousand suns.

It's true: God *is* jealous for you. Insanely jealous. But His jealousy is not like ours, tainted by hate and bitterness. His is a jealousy that will rip apart worlds, worldviews and death itself to reach His beloved – even when that beloved has betrayed Him over and over again. His love is the type that will tear systems and armies and thought patterns asunder to save His child, no matter how long that child has been estranged. By the way, that child – that beloved – is *you*.

God's love is so vehement and violent that he has already sacrificed part of Himself – His only Son – to save you from the pit of your own self-destruction.

I've known people who recoiled in disgust or sneered in disbelief when they heard about God's pursuit of someone who doesn't fit into their mold. "That person's a monster. Why would God have anything to do with him?" "You're trying to tell me God's after her? Do you have any idea the things she's done with her body?" "Why would God show Himself in dreams to Muslims? They're all zealots or worse. And besides, they worship a false god."

Let me ask you: how far would you go for one of your kids?

Well that's *nothing* compared to how far God will go.

God is relentless. And while He will not foist Himself on anybody – He loves you too much to do that – He *will* pursue you. In little ways and in subtle contexts, He will hunt you until the day you die. He will whisper in your ear. He will tug at your heart. He will show you just enough to make you intrigued, wondering if He was really there. And He will offer you a better way.

I wish I could say that all of the pain and problems magically go away when you embrace God's tumultuous, life-giving love. But that's really not what it's there for. It's there to sustain you through the pain. To give you peace when it's naturally impossible to feel any. To fashion you into the man or woman you were designed to be. To overwhelm you with that love when the world around you is lifeless and cold.

But here's what's really staggering. The Bible says that we are supposed to conform to the image of Christ. That means we are supposed to love just as violently as He does.

What does that look like, for us to love with the violence of Jesus? It means we burn with a fervency for people who no one else will look at. For the people who don't fit in our box or our worldview. It means that we doggedly pursue the unpursuable, not because they are a trophy to be collected but because they are a treasure and it's time they saw it. I pray that I can live with that passion that Jesus has – the love that drives us and sustains us even through unbelievable agony and the heights of shame.

I pray that, at the end, it will be said of me that I loved as violently as the God who murdered Himself for us.

Behind Our Masks

You walk into the party. The lights are low and dusky, but you can still easily see them: your fellow party-goers. They mill about, talking, laughing, and you join them. You've spent so much time with them that you call them by name. They're your friends. Your family. But you only know them by their masks.

Some of the masks are beautiful. Some are strong. Some are expensive. Some are chiseled. *All* cover the truth. To show your truth, after all, is the ultimate faux pas.

Just to be certain, you reach up and touch your face. Your mask is firmly in place. Good. Now the evening can begin.

...

We all wear masks. The question is, does yours ever come off?

And, when it does, what lies behind it?

...

I am fascinated by masquerade masks. I think they are wonderful and strange and mysterious. My wife and I have developed a collection of them, in fact — at least of the cheap ones you can buy in most stores around Halloween time. When you put one on, you become someone else. You become some*thing* else. But sometimes that mask can stay on a little too long.

You've probably been fashioning your mask for years. Maybe you're not even sure who you are without it. But underneath it lies the true you. The you that God fashioned and placed on this earth.

Now, you probably don't walk around wearing an actual mask. But, whether through circumstance or intention, you have been creating one nonetheless. Or several, even.

You make one around your job. Then, when people ask what you do (which is another way of asking who you are), you say "I paint houses." Or "I'm an accountant." Often that's as deep as we get with people. We take on that job as our identities, as our main connection to others. But that doesn't even skim the *surface* of who we are.

For five years I was the finance and administration guy. But I was *never* really those things, deep down. I was a poet. A thinker. A philosopher. An evangelist. A theologian. A movie buff. A historian. A tentacle lover (what can I say? They're cool.) A weirdo. A storyteller. But very few knew that, because I didn't tell them. My job became my mask. And that's how people identified me. This wasn't the job's fault: it was mine. I said it was because most of the people I interacted with were tied in with my work, but mostly it was because I wasn't secure enough in who I really was to tell people.

Or take my father-in-law. He is widely identified as a director and tax accountant. But that's what he does. It's not who he *is*. He's a family man. And a painter who prefers watercolors. A person with a deep, abiding care for others. A Star Trek nerd. A man with an overwhelming sense of duty and honor. He is much more than just a number-cruncher. Or "the boss." But very few people know it. They might sense bits of it, but really they focus on his mask. I think occasionally it's hard even for *him* to see what's underneath.

Sometimes how others perceive us becomes a mask. So can our affiliation (or lack thereof) with a given social group. Take my wife. She is perceived as a housewife. Or a stay-at-home mom. She is not often in the "cool" circles – or if she is, it's almost as a "token membership." She has been looked down on because of that. But she is a leader. She is a care-giver. She is a prayer-warrior. She is a wise woman. She can be brutally, bluntly honest. She can transform a person's week by her touch. She is a sculptor. She is kind, and she can be overwhelmed with love for you. She is more than what others have pegged her as. And so are you.

There are many other ways we can create masks. But I'm not going to go over those currently. I'm also not saying that masks are always a bad thing. Jesus had to wear one for thirty years. In fact, His mask didn't fully come off until after He had died. Paul said, "For though I am free from all, I have made myself a servant to all, that I might win more of them. To the Jews I became as a Jew, in order to win Jews. To those under the law I became as one under the law (though not being myself under the law) that I might win those under the law. To those outside the law I became as one outside the law (not being outside the law of God but under the law of Christ) that I might win those outside the law. To the weak I became weak, that I might win the weak. I have become all things to all people, that by all means I might save some. I do it all for the sake of the gospel, that I may share with them in its blessings."[38] Paul had an entire collection of masks, and he rotated through them depending on who he was with. But here's the point: who he truly was, deep inside, always showed through. If you were looking, you could always see what Paul really wanted, or who Jesus really was.

My concern is that we become so comfortable with our masks that we start seeing *ourselves* in that porcelain façade. That it becomes who we are, and the depths we contain are lost. What if we reach the end of our lives, and then realize we were living a half-truth (or worse, an outright lie) for most of it? What if we never allow ourselves to be seen as who we really are?

Your mask is comforting. It is beautiful. It is mysterious. But who you really are is far better. With all your quirks, with all your loves, with all your idiosyncrasies, YOU are worth seeing. You are worth knowing.

Might I ask you to do something for me? Become comfortable with who you are. With who God has made you to be. And, once in a while, let the people see.

The Seattle Journal
Part Two

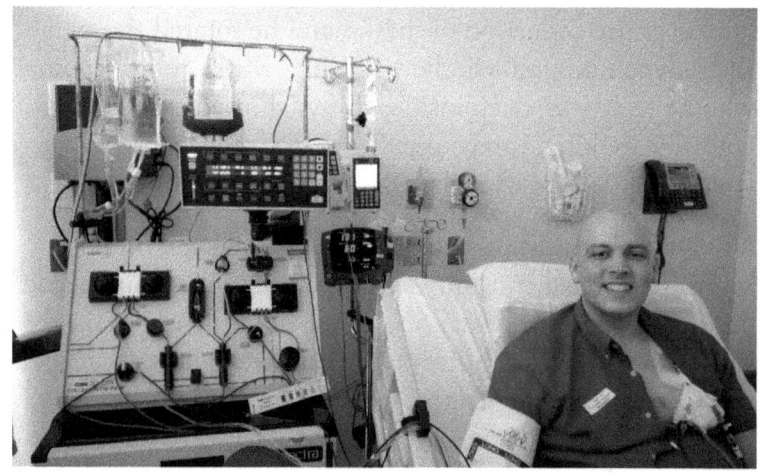

Not long before we headed up north Sarah and her mother, Pam, organized an emergency family meeting. Our whole lives were about to turn upside down, so they figured we should get everyone on board with what was about to happen.

I have to admit, though, that I was strongly against it. Maybe "strongly" is the wrong word, actually. I was adamantly, almost *violently* opposed. On the outside I was cool, composed and collected, but on the inside I felt that in the end only God would be with us. This is not a faith statement. This was because I was bitter, hurting and broken.

I felt people were coming to ogle at us like we were some side show, moan and murmur their condolences, then go back to their normal lives, grateful they weren't us. And then we'd be forgotten, apart from an occasional "Praying for you, brother." So what was the point of giving them their show?

We had the meeting regardless. I was overwhelmed. All-in-all it wasn't a huge group: maybe twenty people total. But the level of love and support people showed us was incredible. Out of that meeting came a framework that would support us over all the months that were to follow. And, within two weeks of that meeting, one couple had said they wanted to donate $500 a month to support our kids, and one incredible man told us he wanted to give us the money to pay for our mortgage for the four months I would be unable to work. But this was just the beginning.

As I mentioned previously, on October 9th Sarah and I drove up to Seattle, as prepared as we could be for the months that were to come. We checked in at the room that would serve as our apartment for the foreseeable future, and then we went to meet our new medical team at the Seattle Cancer Care Alliance.

We met our nurse, Jen, and Dr. Ajay Gopal. We learned some more about the treatment I would be undergoing, were told of the potential experimental treatments I might be eligible for, and realized that the nurses we had talked to on the phone had greatly overemphasized our need to be staying at Seattle right then. Assuming we were willing to commute pretty much daily (including weekends) between

Tacoma and Seattle, we would be able to stay at home — at least for the time being. Since the apartment/room was $100 a night and our girls were in Tacoma, that was a pretty easy choice. But it turned out to be lucky we were there for a few days in any case.

I had been getting daily shots to boost my stem cell production into overdrive. This was all well and good as long as I was taking a Claritin every day. If I stopped, though, my body would feel the wrath of insane stem cell overpopulation. We were having appointments non-stop those first couple days from morning to evening. And it was on day two that I didn't take the Claritin.

I started feeling it mid-morning as a throbbing in my tailbone and between my shoulder blades. It felt a bit like when your back is really out, but with this interesting pulsing sensation accompanying it. Overall, though, I could live with it.

As the day progressed, however, so did the pain. So much so that by mid-afternoon it was staggering. I could barely walk. I couldn't sit. I grit my teeth and bore it through each of our consecutive appointments, and then when we were done I stumbled into the shuttle that would take us back to our room. It wasn't even a pain that I could get used to. It pulsed with the beat of my heart, in and out, in and out; intense, and then cataclysmic.

Somehow I managed to get into the room and collapse on the bed. And that's all I could do. Sarah sat down beside me, and we began to pray. We prayed for the pain to leave, and we prayed that I would be filled with the peace of the Holy Spirit. And then, almost exactly one minute after we started, an amazing thing happened. The pain drained away, leaving only a whisper of its previous screaming. My body relaxed. And I was overwhelmed by peace. I took the Claritin I had missed, rolled over, and slept for several hours. The last of the pain vanished, and it didn't come back.

The following Monday we had our next surprise. My body was still recovering from my last chemo the weekend before, and it was anticipated that I would not be ready to harvest stem cells for another week or two. However, my blood was drawn on Sunday, and when we went in on Monday they told me on their metric I had skyrocketed from a 2.5 to an 8.6. So they performed another test on me, to see how many stem cells I had. I needed at least 10 million, since they were shooting to take 5 million. My test returned: my body contained 89 million stem cells.

Sarah and I went down a few floors and they hooked me up to a machine straight out of "2001: A Space Odyssey" or "Alien." It would suck out just about every cell of blood from my body, whirl it around in a centrifuge, pull the stem cells away and up into a little bag, and then pop the remaining cells (assumedly dizzy and harried) back into my body. I imagine the cells looked something like the illustration included here.

It was not uncommon for people to need several days of this in order to get all of the 5 million cells required for the transplant, though they were fairly confident it would only take one day for me. They were right. When all of my harvested cells were counted, I had given them 30.8 million. (Author's aside: as I wrote this I saw a note I'd written that I might have been wrong on these numbers. But if I was, the numbers were low. Way low.)

So a week ahead of schedule and 25 million stem cells up we moved forward with the battery of tests. When all was said and done, it looked like we were on trajectory to be done with everything and home by Christmas. But then another monkey wrench was thrown into the mix: my doctor told me I had been accepted into an experimental study. Which was great. But the first open slot was partway through December. Which meant that, rather than being home for Christmas, it was looking like we were going to spend Christ's birthday in the hospital. Assuming, of course, that we said, "yes."

Prayer Like Summer Rain

I would like to start this post out with a confession. I have read (or tried to read) many, many books on prayer. I have listened to many, many sermons on prayer. And for some reason most of them have, at some point, rubbed me the wrong way.

I don't know exactly what the problem is. I don't know why I have such a hard time stomaching these treatises on prayer. After all, prayer is the lifeline between you and God. What is there to be so put off by?

That previous statement isn't quite true, though. I have a few rough ideas on what the problem could be. It is always said that the true prayer warrior must wake up at the crack of dawn (or before) to pray for at least two hours at a time. I hate mornings. I think mornings were sent from Satan to torment us. So that is strike one. I think that even more than that, though, it is the way that prayer is often talked about as mandatory ritual. This is not really prayer we're talking about, but Prayer.

We need to Pray. We need to Pray a lot. If we really love God, we will Pray for this many hours a day. If we love God even more, we will Pray faithfully for so many hours a day on weekends. If we are completely devoted to God, we will Pray with Fasting as well. And if we miss our quota of Prayer, we should — nay, must — feel Guilty. And if we happen to see someone struggling with this, it is our job to chide them for not Praying enough, and to Humbly extol our greatness on this particular subject.

On top of this, there's all of the people I've seen who seem content to "pray and see mountains move", but never want to do anything apart from this to see those mountains move. To me this is not faith: it's laziness. And I don't believe God will often answer a person who is not willing to do anything about the thing she prays for. (I'm not speaking, of course, about the things we can never hope to change on our own: all I'm saying is that, as with faith, prayer without works is dead.) The last thing that bothers me about prayer is similar: how often Christians will say to someone, "I'll pray for you." But how often does that person actually pray for the other? How many times is it just empty words so that we look like we care? (This is something I am surely guilty of.)

So, really, my hang-ups don't have anything to do with

prayer at all. They have to do with people, people's biases, and how people treat this most sacred occupation.

When we strip away all of the thoughts people have thought, the beliefs people have enshrined, the dogma people enforce, what do we have left of prayer?

Here's what I feel, deep in my gut. This is what prayer is to me.

Prayer is like a cool summer rain on a blistering hot day. It is a spring of water that wells up inside you and drenches you from the crown of your head to the soles of your feet. Prayer is a centering of yourself, and a death of yourself to live for Someone else.

Prayer is mystical. It opens pathways to a Force beyond anything that we can possibly imagine or contain. Prayer is beautiful. It reveals to us a world of unimagined peace and wholeness and glory. Prayer is your lifeline to the Creator of the universe. Prayer is your way to touch lives you could never otherwise reach.

Prayer – in all its varying forms – is a tool to change the world and the course of history.

Prayer is not dead words or empty repetitions. It is *alive*. It is a breathing, swelling, moving thing. It is poetry given life. And, if you listen very closely, it is also a conversation.

So how do we do this prayer thing? Without compulsion, without guilt, as a genuine and free expression to God? We start by simply engaging in conversation. Tell God what you're thinking. What you're feeling. Ask what He thinks you should do for a given situation. You might not get an answer right away, but slowly you will start to. Whether in words or in images or just in leanings toward a certain direction, you will hear if you listen. If you don't know what to say or need something to get you started, pray the Lord's prayer[39] or one of the Psalms.[40] There is power in the words of the Bible, and doing this can help propel you into that place of peace. As you feel more confident, use the Lord's Prayer as a blueprint, following its basic structure while making the words your own. I still do this quite often, especially starting with praising God and then calling His Kingdom to earth and His will to be done. Two other things that can be extremely effective in getting you into that place of deep peace are reading the Bible and praying in tongues. (If you don't believe in praying in tongues, that's fine. If you want to do it but haven't yet, let me know. I'd be happy to give you some help.)

Once you've started with this, you can expand to other areas like praying for other people. I normally start by asking God to help them, but then I quickly move into the authority that God has given every Christian[41] and start working with God by commanding sickness to leave people or situations to resolve themselves. I have seen this work many times, both in my life and in the lives of others, so I know it works (no matter how strange it may sound.)

But what about timeframe? When should you pray? Whenever you are able to carve out time and feel the most open. I seem to be the most open mentally and spiritually around noon. Having said that, I find myself praying all day long. In the car, walking in the store, at home. I find that I pray best when I'm walking or pacing. It is important to have time just between you and God, but that's not the only time you can or even should pray.

If you're looking for further reading, I highly recommend "The Practice of the Presence of God" by Brother Lawrence. There's a reason this little book from the 1600's written by a monk is still widely available today. It's because it's awesome. "The Circle Maker" by Mark Batterson is also really good, though I'll admit I did struggle through some of my old feelings while reading it.

I realize I've barely grazed the surface on the subject of prayer. But I hope this helped you see that there's more to prayer than a requirement and empty repetitions. It is a living conversation with a very real and living God. Prayer has the power to change your life. It also has the power to change the world.

Why Do You Believe That?

I recently had a very interesting conversation with a young man. We met because he had mocked a belief that I and many others share, so I invited him to talk to me about what his beliefs were on that subject and others. As we talked I learned that he believed that the entire Bible hadn't happened yet and was set at some point in the future, that only one person had ever had the Holy Spirit (the woman who proclaimed the Bible was yet to come, and who was also now deceased), and that God didn't really exist, was some other being, or possibly was this woman (I admit, I was never really sure on that point.)

Sounds kind of outlandish, doesn't it? A little far-fetched?

I believe that a man two thousand years ago came back to life after he was dead for three days. I don't believe that the Holy Spirit just lived inside him: I believe that he literally *was* God. I also believe he did some miracles that bent, broke or shattered the laws of physics, like walking on water. Did I mention that when he came back to life he could walk through walls? That's pretty outlandish, too.

I don't mention this young man's beliefs to ridicule them or belittle him in any way. I mention them for another reason entirely: he had *nothing* to back up his claims. He didn't know why he believed what he believed. He just did, and got remarkably defensive any time I questioned him. He told me repeatedly to stop analyzing what he was saying and just believe.

And there's the rub.

Why do we believe the things we believe? Is it because it's what our parents taught us? Is it because it's what's fashionable? Is it because it's what seems like a good match for us? Maybe we really admire the person doing the telling, and that's enough.

It's so easy to say, "I believe it because it's the truth." Ah, but whose truth? Yours? Mine? Someone else's? Are you so sure there's just *one* truth? What evidence do you have? What proof do you have that yours is *the* truth?

What we believe matters a lot. If we're wrong, after all, the consequences for us and others could be catastrophic. Which is why, in my opinion, *why* we believe is just as important as *what*.

When I was growing up, I belonged to a church that believed it was the only true church (as so many do, deep down inside.) They believed that it was possible many other Christians could be considered "saved," per se, but they were never going to get to the very best place in the afterlife. This was because everyone apart from our church did not have the knowledge of this higher, better place, and so were not eligible for it. While it was vehemently denied that this was the case, the entire system was salvation based on knowledge. Not even on *works*: on knowledge.

I remember vividly a funeral for a friend I attended with other members from this church. He was one of the best men I've known, but I remember people saying how sad it was that he wouldn't reach the eternal home he *could* have had because he didn't *know* about it. We had many other interesting beliefs, too, and I believed them because the people I most respected told me it was true.

Then they kicked me and my family out. And suddenly we found ourselves alone.

I began a journey then. I decided I was God's free man, and that I would learn the truth no matter what form it took and no matter where I had to find it. I spent years in this pursuit. I'm still doing it today. I decided that I would find the glimmers of God and his truth wherever I could find them, and if I found dust and darkness then at least I would know where He was not and how to defend against it.

I read books on science's relation to God. I read "lost" books written by early Christians. I brushed up on Gnosticism. (What a farce that is.) I read (and am still reading) holy books from the other world religions. (Of them, the Tao Te Ch'ing is my current favorite.) I did find glimmers of God, in the most unexpected of places. I realized not just how many differences there are, but what we all have in common. This gave me a tool that I cherish to this day: the ability to listen to people of other beliefs, find the common ground, and reveal how that common ground points them to the one true God. And there's always more to learn. I'm currently working through the Qur'an. Not because I see great revelations of God in it (I honestly don't: it's rather difficult to read), but so that when I meet a Muslim I will be able to converse with him knowledgeably on his religion and show him the pointers toward Truth.

So where am I today and why am I telling you all this? I am in a place that is largely orthodox Christianity, but at the same time it is a very strange, scary place for many Christians. I tell you this because I don't think it should be.

How do we know we have the truth? I believe there is one foundational Truth, but many *don't* believe that. So why do you believe the way you do? Do you actually have evidence for it? Do you believe blindly based on a path whose construction you couldn't begin to guess at? Or do you believe clearly because you have examined the well-established bedrock under your feet?

And did you ever think to glance at people on the other paths to see why they're there?

I'm treading on a path that I know is true because I analyzed it, poked at it, saw what made it tick. I know what's true because I also know what's false. I can defend and share my faith because I can back it up with fact.

Do people always agree with me? No, not even close. Many would consider me aberrant, some would consider me heretical. But I know *why*. And you should, too.

Please don't misunderstand me. I haven't arrived, I don't have all knowledge, and the more I learn the more I realize I don't know. But that's part of the thrill of this life. Why skate by? Embrace it to the full. Use that gray matter God gave you. What you'll end up with is a deeper knowledge of Him, a greater understanding of your fellow man, and the answer to the question, "Why do you believe that?"

Embracing the Mystery

I'm a fan of a line I've heard the evangelist Mario Murillo use: "I love sacred cows. They taste delicious." Today we're going to serve up some sacred cows and see if he's right.

Speaking of which, have you noticed that we are all so sure that we're right? We have spent so many years building our worldview that, when we take a step away to look at it, we don't see the cracks, the missing pieces, the chinks in the façade. Instead our chests swell with pride and we say, "This is mine. And it is right." We don't like it when our fortress is threatened, either, so we wheel out the big guns to defend it.

I've done it. Have you? I bet you have, even if you don't realize it.

Between 1618 and 1648 there was a devastating war called The Thirty Years' War. It was one of the most destructive and bloody wars in western history. This war was carried out for a variety of reasons, but one of the sparks that started it came from the conflict between Catholics and Protestants. Both sides said the other was going to hell, and the early combatants were only too eager to send their opponents there as swiftly as possible.[42]

Why do I bring up this bloody, dark conflict? Am I trying to make Christians feel guilty, as so many others have tried to do? No. Not at all. What I'm trying to show is that, regardless of our belief system, these feelings of rightness and wrongness still abound in our own hearts today. Even if we don't always go to war over them now.

I think this can come down, in a sense, to two different Christian evangelists. One evangelist lives and breathes to show people the love of God, and to help them experience it. The other declares that if you don't follow his belief system then you are going to Hell (probably with his message emblazoned on a large cardboard sign.) What are the big differences between these two men? Obviously, love is a big one. (Though the second would say he does what he does for love.) But the second is what the person is ultimately trying to do. The first is trying to help people, and give them a better way to live. But the second is expounding that his belief system – his particular, nuanced worldview – is the way, the truth and the life.

How many churches decry fellow churches because they worship differently? How many fellow believers spew hate because others think and practice differently? How many times have we condemned others outside of our own group because they were outside?

I heard two people talking recently about baptism. One person said that the physical act of baptism is an essential part of salvation. The other person said baptism was an outward sign of being buried with Christ, but someone could still be saved without it. *Who is right?*

Do deathbed conversions matter? What if a person dies before she is baptized? Are there allowances? What about where the Bible says that "Baptism… now saves you…"?[43] What about Cornelius and his household, who received the Holy Spirit *before* they were baptized?[44]

Some churches speak in tongues. Are they being gripped by an outward manifestation of a demon? Some churches *don't* speak in tongues. Are they devoid of the Spirit and incapable of truly following or experiencing God?

There are churches who say that we are predestined. There are others who say we live exclusively by free will. And they can often turn on each other when these views clash.

I personally have seen too many times when I have known God was guiding something and that it was His plan. I'm going to be honest: I can't imagine how my life would have gone if I hadn't gotten cancer. Many would practically call it blasphemy for me to imply what I just did in that last sentence. But I also know I've made my own choices many times, and that others are waiting for a word from God when God just wants them to *make* a choice.

I've been told many times that I got cancer because of the objects in my house and the darkness in my own life. I've been told I got it because of what I eat, or what I don't eat.

I've been told I got it from my family genetics. I've been told I got cancer because it was God's plan, and I've been told I got cancer because it was the work of Satan.

Who is right?

I heard a radio interview between a young earth creationist and a wonderful man I follow named Hugh Ross.[45] They were talking about the age of the earth and the age of the universe. The interviewer said, "So let me ask you, what does this really matter? In the grand scheme of things, how important is this?" Hugh Ross answered quickly (I paraphrase), "It doesn't. It's just interesting, and it's a wonderful tool to discuss the love of God with other people." His opponent then piped up (I paraphrase again), "I disagree. I believe that everything rides on this, and that if you don't believe this way your salvation is at risk." I could visualize him pulling his cardboard sign out of his backpack.

Why do we hardline on one side or the other of a paradox when the answer is very probably "yep?"

There is mystery in this world. It is all around us. We see through a glass darkly, and we won't cease to do so in this world. Many scientists seek a theory of everything, but should they find it they will then find their bubble pricked by the next great discovery. We can keep on in our surety that we have all of the answers, and that our truth is THE truth. Or we can choose to embrace the mystery. We can choose to judge and be judged, or we can choose instead to love.

When we get to Heaven, I think we will laugh when we see how much of what we held as our most cherished beliefs are straw men and frauds. Why not admit we don't know it all now, and allow that others could have something to add to us rather than opposing us?

As someone who has been on both sides of the divide, I can tell you which side I'm choosing: I choose to embrace the otherworldly, intangible, unknowable Mystery.

"For my thoughts are not your thoughts, neither are your ways my ways," declares the Lord. "For as the heavens are higher than the earth, so are my ways higher than your ways and my thoughts than your thoughts."[46]

"Great is the Lord, and greatly to be praised, and his greatness is unsearchable."[47]

The Seattle Journal
Part Three

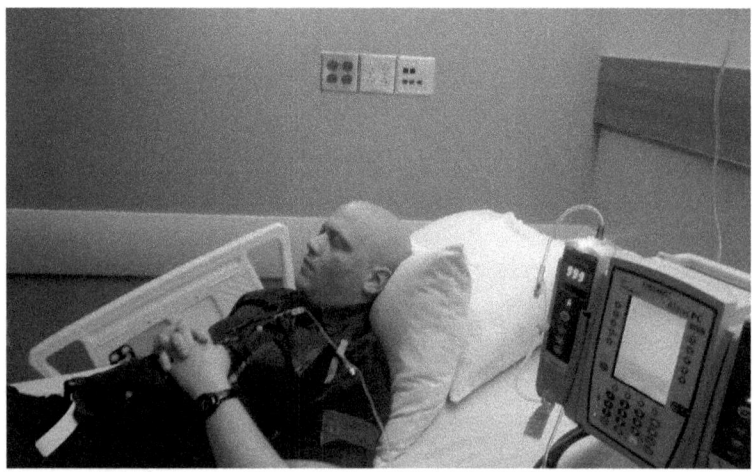

How could I forget to tell you about the tentacular chest dongles?

Before we went up to Seattle, I was told that I needed something put in me called a Hickman central venous catheter. So I went in for a quick surgery, and when I came out there they were: my own pair of tentacles sprouting out of my chest. I'm a huge fan of tentacles, so I naturally thought this was awesome. I immediately started calling them my techno tentacles. But then a few times I also called them my chest dongles. People seemed to really dig the second title, so I combined them. And thus the tentacular chest dongles were named. Between them and my bionic third nipple (also called a power port by those in the medical community who realized its awesomeness,) I was getting closer and closer every day to Robocop. Or at least Doctor Octopus. But I digress.

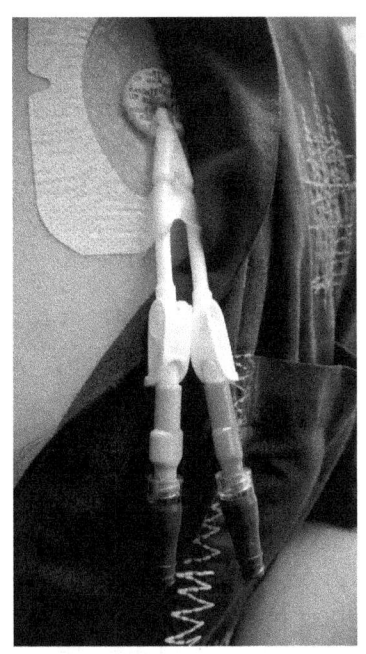

My initial gut reaction to the experimental treatment was "no." I didn't want to be in the hospital over the holidays. I didn't know how we would survive for an extra month or more without income. I had no clue how it would all work. It wasn't until I was talking with my dad about it that things started to click in place for me.

"So they think this will have a better chance of killing the cancer?" he said. I said they did. "And it's only an extra month?" I affirmed. "Well, I don't want to tell you what to do," he said, "but it kind of seems like a no-brainer to me. We'll figure out the money. It'll give you more time to work on your writing projects. It's only one Christmas. And it's not that much more time." I was, in a way, caught up short. He was right. With a little faith for finances, I'd have a better chance of beating cancer. I'd be helping advance medical science for others. And, in theory, I'd have more time to work on what mattered to me. Suddenly I found myself leaning toward yes.

We learned some more about the treatment. Basically they would take antibodies from mice, tweak them into little homing missiles, program them to seek out the cells that surrounded my cancer, attach radioactive isotopes to them, and then inject them into my blood stream. Here's the way I looked at it: I thought of the radioactive antibodies as the mice, my body as the maze, and my cancer as the cheese.

In the end, I said yes. So we began preparation for an even *more* involved treatment.

To start with, we would need to have some chemo in the meantime to tide me over. So we did a third round of ICE after all. This time, though, it was at the University of Washington, not at Saint Joseph's in Tacoma. And *everything* was different. We had become so used to Saint Joseph's, with their nightly prayers and bright white rooms and round windows. The UW, on the other hand, was cramped, dingy, labyrinthine and square. That wasn't the only thing that was different: I found myself experiencing, for one of the first times ever in chemo, sickness from the chemicals.

I suppose that's quite a statement in and of itself. But it was unnerving to suddenly feel nauseated and topsy-turvy after so long of doing so well — including on the exact same treatment regimen. I left those three days feeling uneasy. *How long* was I going to have to be in that place again?

We did make friends during these months, and we were able to touch people's lives. Especially lab technicians, for some reason. We befriended Beau, an awesome Christian guy with an attention span like a squirrel's and a slapstick sense of humor. We also became close with Janice, a sweet lady with a lovely, steady nature and a faithful, deep smile.

I gave copies of the first volume of "The Cancer Diaries" to several people, and it seemed to touch them. (Having said that, without a doubt the best evangelist for the book has been my dad, Chris. My own efforts have paled next to his. He deserves a shout out. =) But it was incredible how much of our time was spent driving back and forth, back and forth. It was practically a full-time job in and of itself.

During this period, however, I did experience another miracle. I had a dead wisdom tooth extracted, and I felt almost no pain at any point amidst the procedure, after the procedure, or in the recovery process. I stopped taking Advil after the first day when I realized it wasn't doing anything. After all of the horror stories I had heard of intense, wailing agony for days, mine passed with barely a whistle. But I was okay with having this expectation dashed.

Could it have just been because the tooth was dead that I didn't have the normal anguish associated with a tooth extraction? Maybe. But I don't think that was all of it. As an aside, the accompanying tooth cleaning hurt far worse than having my tooth ripped apart and suctioned out of my mouth.

Finally we drew up to the main event. Since I didn't know when I'd get out of the hospital, or in what condition I'd be in afterward, I convinced my family to have Christmas beforehand. So we had our daughter Aurora's birthday a week or so early, and then we decided to have Christmas on her birthday, December 7th. (She was totally okay with this arrangement, by the way. It was like two solid weeks of giving gifts to Aurora.) In-between the birthday party and Christmas, though, I had to go in for a test-dose of the experimental treatment. They wheeled in the lead-shielded vial of mouse cells and injected them into my arm. Man, those mice can punch.

I became very sick during the treatment, and spent the next two days sleeping at our friend Colleen's house and fending off fevers. I was trying to avoid the hospital, because that would give our doctors the ammunition they needed to say we couldn't go home for our little Christmas that weekend. I thought I was in the clear, but then I spiked a fever just shy of 103 degrees. I quickly got people praying and prayed in earnest myself. But despite everyone's best efforts we ended up having to go into the hospital anyway. However, by the time we got there the fever had gone down by a degree. By the time a couple hours had passed it had returned to what they considered acceptable norms, so they kicked us out in the middle of the night (around 12:30AM) and we went back to Colleen's.

The next morning I awoke feeling incredibly peaceful. Sarah took my temperature and it was 99.3. By the time we got to the doctor's office again it had plummeted to 98.6. The nurses were shocked. They asked what medications I had downed to get it to drop, but we said I hadn't taken anything because they'd told me not to.

Sometimes God answers our prayers a little late. And it's always better when He does. I got some badly needed fluids at the hospital, and we still ended up being able to go home to our kids. (Though we did sneak out of Seattle a day earlier than we were told we could. My bad.)

We had our Christmas, and we

lived up those few days like we have rarely lived anything up. Sarah even let a new member come to join our family named Brain. She felt sorry for me, and so she was especially weak at the time. Perhaps I should be ashamed of taking advantage of this, but he's just so awesome that I can't be.

But, as all things do, this little bright spot of time slipped away. So Sarah and I once again packed our bags and headed up to the UW in Seattle. Apart from one tiny blip early on, I wouldn't see home again for nearly two solid months.

In the Bleak Mid-Winter
Advent Part One

The wind howls through the stark tree branches colored monochrome by chilled bark and crystalline white. Icicles drape like vines of diamond from ledges and limbs and logs. The world is blanketed by the hush of a fresh snowfall, the stillness thick enough to taste as it presses against the skin and sets hairs on end. No babble from the frozen brooks, no splashing from the icy lake. The world is silent. The world is waiting.

In the bleak midwinter
Frosty winds made moan.
Earth stood hard as iron,
Water like a stone.
Snow had fallen snow on snow,
Snow on snow,
In the bleak midwinter
Long ago.

A whisper sifts through the stillness; a hint of another world brushes against ours. One can almost see the beating of mighty wings in the open air. You squint as the sun glances off a snow bank – or was that a glimpse at Heaven?

Now the wind carries the echo of a voice, inhuman and ethereal: "Holy holy holy! Holy is the Lord God Almighty, who was and is and is to come!" There is the sense of a limitless multitude of eyes, all of them staring, transfixed, unblinking, at a small hovel – a makeshift barn, it seems – halfway carved into a stony hillside.

Angels and archangels
 May have gathered there,
 Cherubim and seraphim
Thronged the air,
But his mother only,
 In her maiden's bliss,
Worshipped the Beloved
 With a kiss.

On closer inspection, the barn is inhabited. Lethargic animals cluster together against the cold. Occasional grunts or lows echo into the stillness as the beasts shift and stir and shiver.

But wait – there is something else. Something strange; beyond belief. A family huddles with the beasts, fending off the bluster with chilled straw and a few tattered blankets. Blood soaks the straw near the doorway and freezes to a red frost. What transpired here? What could have befallen this poor, bedraggled couple?

A bundle near the woman's chest stirs, setting a stray strand of sweat-soaked hair swaying. A newborn lets out a soft, plaintive cry. The woman's exhausted lips flutter into a smile, then, bending down, she kisses her child on his beautiful face. You gasp. She gave birth in here. In the depths of the chill, in the bleakness of the night. It seems as though it was a struggle. It looks like the mother and child barely made it. But, against all odds, they both did.

What can I give him,
Poor as I am?
If I were a shepherd,
I would give a lamb.
If I were a wise man,
I would do my part.
What can I give him?
Give him my heart.

You step closer to the child, approaching delicately so as not to alarm. The parents start, and the father begins to rise. You don't even notice him, though. You fall to your knees in the blood and mud and animal stink. There is something about this newborn. Something that radiates from inside.

He turns and looks at you. You stop breathing. A babe so small could not truly focus on a person: you know that. But his gaze pierces into your soul. The baby raises one tiny hand towards you and touches your face. In the ice and dark and howl you are overtaken by a cascading warmth, a slice of steeped infinity in the confined and calloused void. Tears rupture over the lips of your eyelids as you moan. In one moment, realization dawns: this child, born amidst squalor and cold and night, is meant to save the world. And you are so grateful, because you know with your every fiber that He will succeed.

Angels wreathed in singing,
  Host of heaven adore.
  Star beheld with glory
  That did not shine before.
  Shepherds fear the blinding light,
  Haste to understand.
  In the bleak midwinter
  Peace for child, for man.[48]

I Heard the Bells
Advent Part Two

The snow falls in soft whispers as you crunch down the sidewalk. Cars trundle down the road beside you, windshield wipers swishing, swishing as the drivers clench their black steering wheels with white bloodless knuckles. Breath hisses in ribbons from your mouth, curling up toward the blanket of clouds draped high above.

A sound drifts up to tickle your ears from off in the distance: the ringing of bells. They toll and they chime, their sweet reverberations melding together to form a beautiful Christmas carol. You are drawn to the music, numb hands stuffed in half-filled pockets. It is the old church: the one that has been there longer than anyone can honestly remember. The bells in its belly toll their joyous strains, and as they do a small group of carolers accompany the warm tones. For a moment, just a moment, you are transported to another world, another time. A place where peace on earth could actually exist. And you smile.

I heard the bells on Christmas day
Their old familiar carols play.
And wild and sweet
The words repeat
Of peace on earth, good will to men.

But unbidden they slither into your mind: the dark, twisted little thoughts. You think of the recent school shooting. You think of children battling and dying of cancer. You think of babies being murdered inside of their mothers. You think of Jihadists and rapists and protesters and wars; you think of all of the pain and suffering and hatred and venom all around you every day. Your smile gutters, and in its stead rises the dark twist of a sneer. Peace on earth is a fantasy. A lie. Perhaps it is a wonderful ideal, but it is a wonderful falsehood. How can it exist with such darkness writhing and raging in the heart of man?

How did we get to this place? How did we get here, where innocence is nothing more than a distant memory? Where our leaders are liars and our heroes are fiction? How did we sink so far?

And in despair I bowed my head.
There is no peace on earth, I said.
For hate is strong

And mocks the song
Of peace on earth, good will to men.

You turn to leave and set the church firmly behind you. However, in that moment an elegant, picturesque nativity scene rises out of the blizzard, capturing your eye. And in this pause it seems that the insistence of the bells triples. The hooks of the carolers' songs lodge in your heart. You feel a chill run down your spine, and it does not come from the wonderland all around you. It feels like there is someone near. A Presence, weighty and definite. You cannot help it: you fall to your knees in the snow. God is in this place, and you had not known it.

You see the child lying in the manger, and for a moment it is as if you are transported back in time to the faraway dusty streets of Bethlehem. A star burns in the sky as awestruck shepherds wander in from distant fields. And in that place a light blossoms: a light that, as it grows, rages against the gathering, swelling ebony dark. The light bursts across the nation and then beyond, spreading out, out, driving the gnashing, thrashing night back.

Though at many times it spreads beneath the surface of things and though it often seems like the vile black will finally overtake and smother it, still the light presses on. Though the Stygian bile sometimes appears to infect the light and dim it to embers, the light always burns it away.

And then you realize that this light is people. It is men and women embodying the very essence of God going through all the earth, taking the message of God's own Son and establishing a Kingdom not of this world on the very soil upon which they stand. In every little kindness, in every loving word, in every senseless act of generosity, these bright ones multiply and overtake continent after continent.

Not through conquest. Not through hatred. Not through apathy. Through Love. Through a care that cares nothing for its own being. Through the power of the Living God. Through the message that is, indeed, Good News.

You cry out in shock as tears erupt like steaming tributaries down your cheeks. God is not dead. He lives. He has not left us alone. He is with us. He is active through His hands and His feet and a little whisper beckoning to the light. He loved us, and He loves us still. To say "Merry Christmas" isn't just to look back at the far-distant past: it is to spread His joy, right here and now, and it is to look forward to the day when there finally is peace on earth, good will to men.

> Then peeled the bells more loud and deep
>   God is not dead, nor does He sleep!
> The wrong shall fail,
> The right prevail
> With peace on earth, good will to men.[49]

Advent
Part Three

There are two times a year when mankind as a collective group acknowledges the thinness between our world and another. When we admit there might be more than the eye can behold and the fingers can touch. When we all bask and bathe in Wonder. Those two times are Halloween and Christmas. And of these two, the first cannot hold a candle to the latter.

...

Darkness drapes heavy and expectant over the house. It presses down like anticipation, its tendrils thick and total. But then —

A match strikes. In the pendulous night, a single candle springs alight.

. . .

She sits alone on the frigid sidewalk, the wind biting into her face and hands as it whips through her ragged clothes. She is cold. So cold. Christmas lights burn in the distance, and she finds herself staring at them, mesmerized, wishing they burned a little warmer.

The tip-tapping of shoes echoes down the street. She doesn't bother a glance.

"Excuse me," a soft voice falls. "Would you mind if we gave you this blanket? And some soup?"

She looks up, mouth agape. And in that moment she feels the warmth of something greater than herself.

. . .

Another candle lights. And another. And another.

. . .

He sits alone in a hospital room, clinical white and sterile effects. He is trapped in this place. His prison features large windows that look down on a street he can't set foot on while an IV drip chains him to the wall. He knows he won't be home for Christmas. And in this moment the loneliness overwhelms him.

A knock comes at his door. He looks up. "Yes?"

A man dressed in winter clothes pokes his head in the room. "Excuse me, sir. May we come in for a minute?"

"What for?" he says. "Oh, I suppose so."

The man smiles, and then he and three other people shuffle into the room. They are carrying hymnals. "We thought," he said, "since you couldn't go out to Christmas, Christmas should come to you." And then they begin to sing.

The man finds that words cannot escape his throat. He determines to hold the tears at bay, but they will not be contained.

...

Another candle lights. And another. And another. And another.

...

The children sit alone in the living room. Mommy and Daddy won't be home this Christmas. They know that now. They had so hoped, but now there is none remaining. Did Mommy and Daddy abandon them? Do they not love them any more?

There is a rapping outside. The doorbell rings.

Tentatively the oldest child works her way down to the front door and peers through the peephole. Frowning, she opens the door.

"Merry Christmas!" cries her family members and neighbors and friends. They burst into the house, bundling in gifts and food and beauty.

The children cannot contain their shock. But the greatest gift of all is when their aunt pulls out a tablet, and on it is an image of their mommy and daddy. "Hello, my sweeties," the mother says softly.

...

Another candle lights. And another. And another.

...

He sits alone on the hard ground, surrounded by tormentors. With inhuman force they thrust him flat against the cold, unyielding earth, pushing him onto the splintered wood. Taking his hands and feet, they drive thick iron nails into his soft flesh, shattering the bone underneath. He cries out in pain as his blood runs like tears.

They pull the cross into the air, sending shrieks through his nerves as the base crashes down into its hole. There were rumors once that he was the messiah. The hero. That he was perhaps even born of a virgin. That he was, in some mysterious way, God walking among his people. But now he is murdered with common criminals.

"My Father, my Father," he moans. "Why have you forsaken me?"

But in that moment his gaze is transported to the future: to far-off times and different lands, where His sacrifice, His message of love, His gift of grace and mercy, is manifested around the world. Whether in little ways or in big, He sees people taking up His name to partake in wanton, random acts of kindness. And, through all of the pain, through all of the hatred and horror, it makes Him smile.

"It is finished," He says. And the world gasps.

...

The final candle is lit.

Advent has ended. Christmas has arrived.

The light of the world walks among us, just as He did over 2,000 years ago.

The darkness is expelled. All we have to do is see it.

God bless you. Merry Christmas, my friend.

The Seattle Journal
Part Four

My first official treatment was the real dose of the experimental procedure. They rolled out the red carpet for it, too. The nurse spent hours readying the room prior to my arrival. Almost every conceivable surface was covered in plastic, paper and tape. It looked a bit like a room in a sanitarium. Eventually they rolled in another lead-lined container, this one substantially larger than the last one. Inside it was a huge syringe filled with Yttrium-90-laced mouse antibodies.

They plugged me in and pumped me full, then wheeled the contraption back out of the room. I felt fairly certain I was well on my way to becoming a superhero or growing an extra appendage of some kind. This feeling was confirmed when a man came in carrying a Geiger counter that he carefully, repeatedly swept over my limbs and torso. As I heard the machine make it's incessant crackling sound, I felt assured I would be getting my third eye at any point over the next few days. That, my friends, is a win.

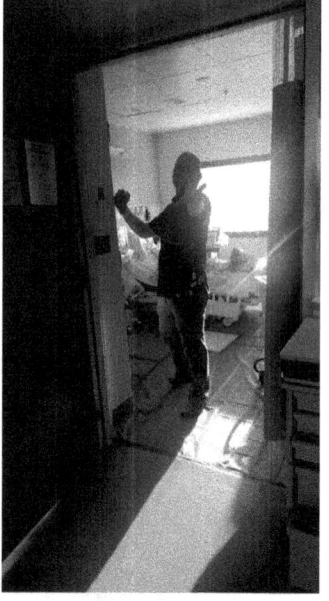

As I prepared to leave the following afternoon, people gathered in the hallway to say hi to me. There's an episode of "The Simpsons" where Mr. Burns is irradiated and has a strange medical procedure done that makes his eyes huge and his voice really high pitched. As Homer runs off screaming, Mr. Burns squeaks, "Don't be afraid. I bring you love." That was totally me.

I blessedly didn't have the side effects with the real dose that I did with the test dose, but I did leak radiation from my sweat and other fluids for several days and so tried to isolate myself as much as possible. However, as the radiation faded, we snuck down to Tacoma to soak up a couple more days with our kids. On a

whim we went to Zoo Lights, and I spent every second trying to burn memories into my brain.

Then the day came to check in for chemo. They pumped me full of lethal chemicals for a solid week and literally killed my immune system, bone marrow and blood cell production. Ironically, they probably weren't killing any cancer at this point, as I had just gotten a PET scan that showed I was clear and clean. (But that's actually just the way they like it. The success rate is far higher when there's nothing much for the poisons to kill.)

We had a problem early on with the chemo when my chest around my tentacular chest dongles began to burn. I called the nurse, and everyone started freaking out. They switched the chemo over to my bionic third nipple, then had a nurse come up and yank out my dongles. Literally. The girl snipped the stitch, wrapped her hands around the tentacles, and pulled. I so wish I could say I felt it slithering out, but I honestly didn't feel much. However, I was definitely aware that my awesome tentacles were leaving me, and that filled me with a deep, soulful sadness. At least until I finally talked the nurse into letting me keep them.

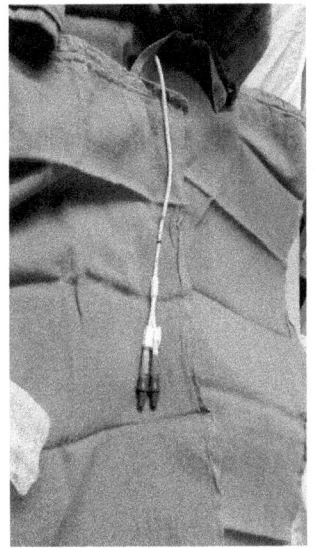

After the chemo I had a day of rest, which they screwed up by implanting another pair of tentacular chest dongles. I never got as attached to these as I did to the previous pair. They were much longer, and more of a nuisance. But they were necessary for what came next.

The following day was Christmas Eve, and it was the day I got a new immune system. They hooked my new dongles up to a bag full of stem cells, and soon the room was steeped in the pungent smell of creamed corn. (No, seriously. That happens with bone marrow transplants.) Within a couple of hours, the stem cells had all been let loose in my body.

There were a number of times that I almost got out of the hospital, but every time something arose to keep me in. The person in charge was Dr. Mohamed Sorror, a very gentle, quiet man with almost no sense of humor and an awesome bow tie. He was also very conservative. Each time we thought I'd get out, he kept me in. I ended up being in the hospital for almost a solid month.

Christmas passed, and so did New Year's. There were fireworks over the Space Needle that we could see from my room on New Year's Eve. Sarah went down to be with the girls for Christmas and a few days following, giving them the incredible Christmas present of their missing mommy. My sister, Dawn, came up to visit Christmas night, giving me the gift of company.

The hardest part of the whole ordeal was the separation from our children. Eventually the girls did come up to visit me, but it took them a long time to warm up. Especially Eden. Not only had I abandoned them, but I was basically stuck in a bed with a myriad of tubes snaking out of my body. I was scary. And because I was so desperately tired much of the time they just had to sit there quietly as the unsettling medical experiment dozed.

It soon became apparent that I have an insanely high pain tolerance. One major side effect caused by this treatment is that it kills the cells in your tongue, mouth, throat and stomach, giving you nausea and vicious mouth sores. I thought I was doing pretty well with the treatment because my pain wasn't absolutely crippling. Nurses and doctors would hear that, start celebrating, and then look in my mouth. They would then say, "Gah!" and jump away in horror. I thought they were just being dramatic. So I looked in my mouth. I jumped back from the mirror, yelling, "Gah!"

My tongue had swollen to fill most of my mouth, and everything in it was bright white and bleeding. No, they weren't being dramatic. I was asked repeatedly, "How are you not on a constant morphine drip?" I would shrug and reply, "Well, my half of an oxycodone is doing just fine for the most part." They would then back out of the room, shaking their heads. I told Dr. Sorror that one day, and he fixed me with a flat, uncomprehending look. "I've never heard of someone taking only half an oxycodone," he said. It was at this time I decided my next career should be fire walking.

As the days passed, though, it became apparent why we were there for such a long period of time. Sarah was spending a lot of time on the next floor up in a little family room they had there, and she was making friends with many, many hurting people. All of them were in desperate need of comfort, love, and a touch from God.

Holy Ghost

How futile this life can be.

We go about our day-to-day activities, scraping for some glimpse of meaning. We cover up the emptiness that carves out our insides with things that are ultimately as empty and useless as what we initially covered up.

"Vanity of vanities," says the preacher. "All is vanity."[50]

To paraphrase the book of Ecclesiastes, in the end everything is dust. Everything is a striving after wind. Whether we build up great wealth or eek out a meager poverty, in the end we will probably go out the way we came in: screaming, naked and alone. All that we have built will ultimately go to someone else. Every memory of us will eventually fade to gauze, and then to nothing. Whether we were monsters or angels, whether we changed the world for good or for ill, how will we ever know what comes after, or the part we really played? What do our actions actually matter?

What's even worse is that, depending on our worldview, this might be all we get. If we are atheists, if we are agnostics, if we are Taoist, if we even lean toward Buddhism or Hinduism, outside of this world all of what makes us "us" will dissolve into the vast quantum ocean.

But there has to be more. There has to be more than this cold. Than this emptiness. There has to be more than the daily grind that rubs us until it has taken all that we are. Are we really just living for "the golden years?" Do we truly just exist for our paychecks and filling our bellies? Even if we live to better others — our family, our children, our spouse — how can we even then escape the plunge down the endless muddy spiral to oblivion?

Everything decays. Friendships, bodies, jobs, the world, the universe. If we live for this life we are grasping for sand that will ultimately pour through our fingers. We need to touch something outside of this material existence in order to grasp anything permanent. We need a Friend who is deeper than death. We need a Holy Ghost.

Maybe you think that I have now stepped into the realm of useless hyperbole. Maybe I am just speaking in dead religious terms about dusty outdated ideas. Maybe we should throw it all out and embrace the true core of this reality: nihilism. The striving after wind. It's what most of the philosophers and great thinkers who rejected God throughout history did.

But there's nothing academic about this. The Holy Ghost is real. I've met Him. And you can, too.

There's an old Christian adage that when you accept Jesus as your savior the Holy Ghost comes and lives inside you, and you become a new person. This is called the "born-again experience." However, I honestly have a hard time saying that a great number of Christians have ever really met the Holy Ghost – or at least actively know Him (especially in the western world.) If they had/did, Christianity would not be in the state it is in today. The Holy Ghost – one person of the fathomless, timeless, boundless God who created this whole universe – is a force beyond this world. And when you meet Him, He changes you forever. When you really and truly experience Him, there is no going back. Why? Because you wouldn't want to.

There is a limitless fire that wants to come and live in your body. There is an unquenchable love that wants to overwhelm your hate and your apathy. The Eternal wants to call you Friend. A bottomless Life wants to fill your deadly emptiness. How do I know this? Because He wanted to do it for me, and He did. He has overwhelmed me with an unspeakable peace and drowned me in deepest depths of joy. He's done it for countless others throughout history, too.[51] But He doesn't stop there at that first time: He wants to do it new and afresh every single day. All we have to do is ask Him to do it.

This is why some people can regularly pray for two hours without stopping: it's because they've gotten hooked. They get to the point where they need their daily fix. They need that peace, contentment and joy new and afresh. And they know that the Holy Ghost is the dealer who always delivers.

So how do you get to meet this Holy Spirit? You ask Him to come and fill you. Even if He already lives inside you, ask for a new filling. Ask Him to make Himself *real* to you. And then sit down, be still, and see what happens. I bet it will change your life.

When the Eternal makes His home in your mortal structure of meat, you will find that you don't just get Him: you get love, joy, peace, hope and more besides. You will know that you are Never Alone. That there truly is purpose to this existence. And you will find yourself, little by little, becoming that new person. Why? Because the God of the universe has just added Himself to you. How could you help but do anything else?

Is the world cold and cruel and callous? It can be. But we have a comforter. We have a help. We have a friend. And He just so happens to be the God of this universe and beyond.

In Our Ruins

When I was very young, my grandfather died in a car accident. Well, that's not entirely true. He actually *survived* the car accident. But he did not survive the medical care that followed.

To my understanding, some thought there were grounds for a medical malpractice suit. Some said it should all just be left alone. But *everyone* agreed that he had gone much too early.

I don't have very many memories of my grandfather. Really

only one (though it is a good one.) But I am told he called me Lord Byron, that he gave me cans of soda to carry around when I was learning to walk, and that he was one of the best men that those who knew him have *ever* known. And when he was gone, he left an enormous hole.

. . .

The book of Ruth opens in a desperate but hopeful journey: as a vicious famine ravaged his homeland, the Israelite Elimelech uprooted his wife, Naomi, and their two sons to take refuge in the faraway land of Moab. Though they were strangers in a foreign country they settled down and began the process of building a home for themselves. The sons, Mahlon and Chilion, fell in love with local Moabite women named Orpah and Ruth and were soon married.

Things were going well, and they were happy. But then tragedy struck. Elimelech died, leaving his family to fend for themselves. They were all devastated, though none more so than Naomi. However, the family pressed together, and they continued on for another ten years.

One could think that this family had been through enough pain. But it was not to be. In one terrible blow both Mahlon and Chilion were cut down in their prime, leaving the three women widowed and alone.

Naomi was beside herself with grief. First her husband, *but now her two sons as well?* Sick of Moab's heartache, Naomi gathered a few possessions, sold the rest, and purposed to return to her hometown of Bethlehem.

Naomi released her daughters-in-law to return to their families, bidding them tear-streaked farewells. Orpah fell on Naomi, kissed her on her cheek, and prayed she have a blessed life. But Ruth staunchly refused. "May the Lord do so to me and more also if anything but death parts me from you!" she declared. Naomi shook her head, but she did not have the energy to fight her. So the two women set out.

...

I learned this week that a friend of mine, a dear lady named Bev Marshall, had died a day or two earlier. I was shocked. We had never met in person, but we had corresponded every week or two for the past six months. We had been going through this cancer thing together. And then she was gone.

My loss, though, is nothing compared to those who knew her deeply: her husband, her family, her dearest friends. That citadel she had built as her life imploded in one final breath, and those who shared it with her are now left picking up pieces that will never fit together properly again.

...

The journey was long and trying. But eventually Naomi and Ruth made it back to Naomi's homeland of Bethlehem. There she was initially greeted with joy, but that joy faded when her friends and acquaintances saw that Elimelech, Mahlon and Chilion were all conspicuously absent.

"Do not call me Naomi (which means pleasant); call me Mara (which means bitter), for the Almighty has dealt very bitterly with me," Naomi replied when they greeted her. "I went away full, and the Lord has brought me back empty. Why call me Naomi, when the Lord has testified against me and the Almighty has brought calamity upon me?"

And so Naomi and Ruth settled in Bethlehem penniless, hopeless, and husbandless. Two widows, one a foreigner in a strange land, both broken people whose worlds had been fractured beyond repair. There were no pieces to even pick up: there was only the wearied tenacity to press on.

...

How often do we find ourselves picking up the pieces? How often does home just not fit us any more? Or, even worse, doesn't *exist* any more? When it seems that all we have worked for, all we have striven for, the life we have so carefully erected, has come crashing down like our own personal Babel? When that person who defined us, who upheld us, who gave us strength, who loved us, isn't there any more? The absence can be so palpably heavy that it can crush us.

In the ruins it can be so easy to see only the bitterness. To be overcome with the overwhelming weight of Loss. To pronounce yourself Mara. To think over and over again "Why?", and to feel cursed by God. It is even easy to curse Him right back.

...

Near Bethlehem there lived a man named Boaz. He was a distant relative of Elimelech, as well as a virtuous, honorable man. He took notice of Ruth and the brave, kind deeds she had done for Naomi. And he treated her with kindness in return: he heaped food on her, enough for the two women to eat for weeks. Ruth worked in his fields gathering until the end of the harvest, and she saw how this man operated. And something bloomed inside her.

At the end of the harvest Ruth came to Boaz in the night and made a bold gamble. She asked him to marry her and to redeem her family. Boaz was taken by her tenacity, and honored by the fact that she had not gone after a man of her own age. So he sought the approval of the elders and the other family members.

The next time Ruth saw Boaz, he had news. He told her that she was to be his wife, and that her family would be redeemed from poverty and tragedy. They were married, and they had a son.

Ruth handed her baby boy to Naomi, and Naomi saw in that newborn's face the smile of her sons, and the piercing gaze of her husband. And at that moment she knew, as tears rolled down her face and laughter bubbled up from her belly, that God had not left her, after all.[52]

. . .

We each have ruins in our hearts, our minds, our memories. We each have the arid places of desolation: where once there had been life and happiness, but now there is only char and wreckage. Sometimes those ruins are all we see. Sometimes they're all we will allow ourselves to see. And so often the question arises, "Why?"

"Why, God? Why me? Why her?"

The desolate places wrench our heart and break us in pieces and sometimes trap us under grief. But God can restore even that which can never be. God can build metropolises out of our ruins that bring in others who would never have been invited in otherwise. He can use our ruins to send us on a journey that will change us and everyone around us forever. (Ruth's son was the grandfather of David, after all.)

Or perhaps He will only use that painful, hulking wreckage as a shelter to grow a single rose, just for you. A tribute to the things and people you've lost, and to the person you have become. We might not even see the rose for a very long time: years, perhaps. But, oh, when we do finally see it, how beautiful, how magnificent that rose will be.

The Art of Human Being

Have you ever felt you are so far behind that you will never catch up?

I have. In fact, I feel that way a lot. That I am losing more ground than I'm covering. That everything just slips farther and farther away, and I can't move fast enough to catch the target.

It's confession time. I'm not just writing this entry today for you. I'm also writing it for me. I guess I write many of these essays for me in some way or another, but today *I* need to hear this. I just hope you do, too. I know a lot of people approach their messages and talks from a place of strength. I've just never found that to be very effective, or very me. So here is my weakness. May we see the strength of God through it.

I fear I am dangerously close to becoming a human doing, and not a human being. Even when I am stopped and relaxing, I am beginning to tighten up because I know there are so many things I need to do. As such, I do not truly stop. And I do not truly relax. And inside I wind up tighter and tighter, because I am not doing what I need to be doing.

Every time I get a burst of traction, too, it feels like a hundred hands reach out to pull me back. Whether it's my health, an obligation I have to fulfill for another person, a person who needs my presence, energy and being, or just the grueling seepage of time, there are many things that conspire to catch me.

Can you relate? Maybe your problem isn't the same. But have you felt that tightening in your chest? That sinking sensation? The impression that, despite your best efforts, you're about to drown?

It might not be a full-on panic attack. It might be a subtle thing, just out of view, that you feel in your belly as it creeps about inside. You're drowning. Your lungs just don't know it yet.

When this happens, what do we do to stem the tide? What *can* we do, against a force so powerful and implacable?

I realize that I must give up control. I must learn to be.

I close my eyes, take a deep breath, and submerge myself in the limitless depths of God. I can feel Him closing around me, encircling and overwhelming me, and as He does He pushes the rest back. The tightness, the darkness, the sense of do, do, do. I trust Him, that He has a plan, and that that plan is good. I trust that, if I keep chipping away day after day, I will eventually bring down a mountain. And I resolve that I will not be consumed by the doing when it returns (as it surely will.)

Because I am a human being.

It's about the little moments. The oddball instances with your spouse and children and siblings and parents. The times that, as you walk away, you realize that you did a good thing, even if it cost you in time and resources and yourself.

In the end, we are all meant to be a human being. Being together. Being in touch. Being connected to someone else and some*thing* else. Being sacrificial. Being giving. Being vulnerable. Being human.

This human experience is our lot, and we shirk it at our own peril. If we allow half of our title to slip away from us, how long before the human part does as well? The doing is a big part of our experience, but so is the being. So, sometime this week, let's unplug. Let's disconnect. Let's pull loved ones close. And let's just be.

The Seattle Journal
Part Five

While I was in bed with mouth sores, Sarah was one floor up in the hospital's little family room ministering to families. She met Matthew and learned about his sister. She became friends with Barb and was eventually introduced to her daughter, Karen. She grew to know Michael and his family. And she was reunited with Pam, who gave her an update on her husband, Bob.

Sarah laughed with them. She cried with them. She

prayed with them. But, most of all, she loved them and showed them hope.

I met Barb right before Christmas and had the opportunity to pray with her for Karen and to give her a copy of my original "Cancer Diaries." Karen was about to go through a double cord-blood transplant. It was a longshot, but Barb was hopeful. It seemed we both had a long road ahead.

I finally reached the point where they had to get nutrients in me with a big bag full of yellow liquid that looked like… Well… I won't say exactly what it looked like among polite society. Also, on general principle they stuck me with a morphine drip after I mentioned the pain in my throat had increased. The morphine didn't help my throat much more than my oxycodone had (which did eventually get up to one whole pill), but it was fun to have a button, and it made them feel better.

People had been saying how well I was doing the whole time, and there had been many occasions, as I mentioned before, where we had heard rumblings about me getting out. The rumblings never panned out. But, finally, doctors and nurses started talking about it and meaning it.

As I was getting better, though, Karen was getting worse. She'd had her transplant, but then several setbacks cascaded into each other and undid everything the treatment had set out to accomplish. It was a crushing blow. Barb and the doctors wanted to keep going, but the glimmer of light Karen had been clinging to was too far away now for her to see. She was utterly exhausted.

It wasn't long before Karen told her doctor that she was done fighting. The doctor pushed back some, but soon he conceded to her wishes. And so the medical staff and her family started trying to make her comfortable as she waited for the end.

Sarah had been feeling like she needed to go up and see Karen, but she hadn't wanted to intrude on their privacy. I told her she needed to just head there and do it. But then the news we had been waiting for arrived: Doctor Sorror came in and told me I would finally be able to check out. Sarah scrambled upstairs to gather her things and I started packing. Some time passed, and I had squirreled away about as much as I could. Sarah still wasn't back. So, to pass the time, I made the mistake of looking at a YouTube video I had been intending to watch, called "Moving On" by James.

I had seen that the story was told with yarn puppets, which I thought was inventive. But what I didn't know was that it depicted a person dying in the hospital while his loved one tried to keep him there. Perhaps needless to say, it completely wrecked me.

Why was I getting out of the hospital when so many others were staying in? Why was *I* getting better when Karen was one floor up slipping farther and farther away? I began praying in anguish for her and for the others, asking God to touch them and give them peace. I wept, and I prayed.

Sometime later Sarah returned, and she was glowing. I asked what she'd been up to, and she told me that she had gone to see Karen. Upon entering the room she met Karen's husband, Dan, in addition to seeing Barb and Karen again. She had prayed with them, and she had delivered the peace I had prayed for. It was some time before I could stop my tears. The next day Karen passed away.

We were released from the hospital, and with a feeling of elation escaped down the street to a comfortable little apartment minutes away. The first thing I remember doing was taking a bath in a real tub, and the second thing was going out to a Thai restaurant.

Why would I do this, you ask? With no immune system, a shrunken stomach and a mouth that was still raw, in a city I didn't know to a restaurant that I'd never been to? The answer is simple: because I could. And it tasted... like dirt. That wasn't the restaurant's fault, though. *Everything* tasted like dirt. Textures, consistencies, flavors, they were all dirt. (Liquids were mud.)

Time passed in our quaint little lockdown. I discovered I was not, nor could I ever be, a Seattlite. I was enlightened to the fact that SyFy channel is the only reason to have cable. We learned how to do IV infusions at home. Then *I* learned how to get over IV-induced nausea. Our girls came to visit us and stayed for a few nights. Those were bright days with them.

Barb and Dan got out of the hospital, raw and numb at the same time. Barb needed to get out of the apartment, the city and the state, so we helped her pack up and drove her to the airport. She was so grateful for the help, and we cried with her and hugged her as she headed into the terminal, scarred but strong. We were able to help Dan as well, in his turn. But then it seemed like weeks passed where we weren't really doing anything, and we started to get frustrated. Why were we still in Seattle if there was no one else left to help?

The day we were leaving I got my answer when I met Debbie. She was about to go through my exact same procedure and was scared of the unknown that lay ahead. She was a Christian, and I had the opportunity to pray with her as I shared my story. Being able to help her made those weeks worthwhile, and aiding those three made Seattle bearable.

In the last days of January they released us. They took out my second pair of tentacular chest dongles, we said goodbye to the friends we'd made, and then we packed up and headed back south. Do you have any idea the feeling of exultation possible over the course of a simple one-hour drive? Or the elation that can overcome you at turning down a driveway? Our adventure was much more mundane than Frodo's or Sam's or the other great questing heroes, but it was our adventure, nonetheless. And we were changed through it.

Though that is technically the end of the story, there is one more detail I must mention. Because, even though the story ended, life (as it does) went on. And there is one miracle that, during the adventure, I have touched on but not elaborated about.

In the time before, during, and after the hospital, one thing we never had to worry about was money. I was unemployed, with no source or real hope of income. But God, through the use of wonderful, giving people, saw that our needs were not only met but exceeded. During that time we had a mortgage and rent (which was two-and-a-half times the mortgage,) hundreds (if not thousands) in travel costs, regular bills, Christmas, sizable medical bills, and other expenses as well. They were all paid for. Through people just like you.

But, as I mentioned, that was a part of the *story*. And

then it ended. We still had several months covered, but eventually the money started to run out – and I still wasn't able to work.

We reached our last $300. Tension started to build. But then, just when the stress was threatening to crack us, I decided that enough was enough. Casting aside all of the fear, I prayed to God, and thanked Him that He was our provision. *He* was our source. I thanked Him that our every need was covered, and that He would supply for us.

That night, we were invited to Panera for dinner. We declined, saying we should save the money as things were starting to get tight. Plus our dryer had just broken, and Sarah mentioned she wasn't sure how we'd fix it. To my knowledge that is all that was said.

The next day an email went out from someone that we were out of money and in need of help. The day after that a family member stopped by and dropped off $1,000. The day after that some dear friends left an envelope with $500. And then we learned that some other friends, the ones who had volunteered to support our kids with $500 a month, wanted to sell some stock and give the money to us. A few days later Sarah's mom stopped by with a check from them for $5,000. I ask you: *does God answer prayers today?*

I used to see miracles in everyday life, maybe more so than many. But now I see that *every day* is a miracle. Both figuratively and literally. We live off of miracles, my family and I. We wouldn't survive without them. I still live in that place of complete natural uncertainty, and, honestly, I'm starting to think it's the only way to go. It is, ironically, the safest place to be.

Einstein couldn't have been more right when he said that "There are only two ways to live your life. One is as though nothing is a miracle. The other is as though *everything* is a miracle."[53] Every day we're alive is a day to be grateful. And so, too, is the day we die. Yes, that's the day our earthly book ends. But it is just the beginning of the grand story we will partake in.

How about you? What's your story? Ah, don't give me that. You do have one. The only reason I thought I had one was because I had the eyes to see it. But I see yours, too. Your life is special. Your actions have meaning and purpose. And God is in it, whether you see Him and His miracles or not. Maybe it's time to see your story. Maybe it's time to see the miracles. Maybe it's time to start living as though everything is.

We Are Reborn

"This must be what it feels like when you begin to die."

That thought hit me one day when I was sitting alone in my room in the hospital. It wasn't a melancholy thought: it wasn't despairing. It was more of a stop-breathing, "whoa" moment. Because it was true.

I had just finished a week-long stint of a lethal chemo conditioning, preceded by an experimental radiation treatment. I say "lethal" because this was not a dose that the human body could survive without immediate and radical medical intervention: my bone marrow had been eradicated, my blood cells had been decimated, and without an injection of stem cells the rest of my body would shortly follow suit.

Thus, a day or two after the last chemo, I wasn't just being dramatic about my condition: I really *was* dying inside.

. . .

One night Jesus was awakened by a Pharisee who crept in to see Him under the cloak of darkness. This holy man's name was Nicodemus, and he wanted to question Jesus away from the prying eyes of his fellow Pharisees.

Jesus completely sidelined the conversation, though, by telling this man that he needed to be born again to inherit the Kingdom of God. Nicodemus, like many others throughout history, was thoroughly confused.

"How can a man enter a second time into his mother's womb?" he asked.

. . .

In the hospital with me was a woman named Karen. My wife, Sarah, and Karen's mother, Barbara, became fast friends. Barbara was believing against all hope that her daughter would survive, but as the days drew on Karen became sicker and sicker. Every direction they turned the doctors seemed to hit a brick wall. Finally Karen said that she was tired of fighting. So the doctors changed gears and started trying to just make her comfortable.

. . .

Jesus told Nicodemus that unless we are born again of water and Spirit we can in no wise enter the Kingdom of God. He said that what is spirit and what is flesh are categorically different. Their conversation continued on, but it is not mentioned what Nicodemus finally came to think.[54]

...

Over the course of a week my old immune system died. In the days that followed, a new immune system was born. I look the same. I sound the same. I act the same. But I am not the same. Fundamentally, I am a different person. A new person. I am starting the new year with what so many desire: a fresh start. It came through pain and hardship and losing 30 years' worth of immunity. But it came nonetheless.

On the day we were set to leave the hospital, Sarah went up to see Barbara, Karen and Karen's husband, Dan. Both Sarah and I had been praying heavily for Karen and her family. I had tried to post an emergency prayer update to my website for her and a couple of others, but every time I tried my site crashed. This and a growing dread both Sarah and I felt brought about the uncomfortable suspicion that we weren't in Karen's life to help her recover.

So, hours before we were set to leave the hospital, Sarah went up a floor to Karen's room and asked if she could pray with her. They were all very receptive and welcoming, even though they were exhausted, quiet and preparing for the end. Sarah knelt over Karen's bed, love in her eyes, and began to pray. She told Karen that God was telling her that He wanted her to say "Yes" to Him, and that she would know what that meant. Karen couldn't speak any more. All she could do was hiccup, open her eyes and softly moan. But what she could do, she did.

Sarah told Karen and her family how much they were

loved, by us and by God. It was a holy moment. And then she left.

When Sarah returned to our room, she told me what had happened. I burst into tears. I didn't know that she was going to see Karen and her family, but almost the whole time she had been gone I had been praying in anguish for these people, pleading for God to touch them. And He did.

A couple of hours later we left the hospital. About one day after that, Karen did, too.

...

How can a person return to his mother's womb? How can we be born again?

How can we look the same, act the same, talk the same, but be fundamentally different people?

I have never before experienced such a clear analogy between the new man and the old one, nor do I expect to again. Not everyone will go through the things I have, nor would I want them to. But perhaps, in looking at my situation, we can all see the rebirth that is accessible to each of us in our inner man. What happened to me physically can happen to *everyone* spiritually.

I've certainly experienced that rebirth of the soul, as well. In fact, I feel like I've experienced that rebirth over and over again, as I grow to know God deeper. Each time is like hitting the reset button. Each time is like a new beginning, with a past that informs but is also distinct. There is Before, and there is After. And to go back would be, in most cases, beyond question. This rebirth doesn't require deadly chemo, mouth sores and nausea, but it does often come with its own unique growing pains. You sacrifice something when you are reborn. Sometimes it's a substance, sometimes it's a way of thinking, sometimes it's the people who kept you in that place of darkness (at least for the time being.) It hurts to be reborn. But the rewards are incomparable.

Having said all of that, I think Jesus was discussing two distinct things when He was talking with Nicodemus. I absolutely know He was describing a here-and-now rebirth, but I also think He was talking about another one as well: when we cast off these earthly shackles and stand anew, afresh, and astonished before Him. When all of the pain, discomfort and darkness suddenly makes sense. When, to paraphrase C.S. Lewis, even our darkest hour becomes light.

As we move into this new year, my prayer is that we would all be able to say that we are starting anew, washed in the blood of Jesus and lit by the Holy Spirit's marvelous flame.

For Karen. For myself. For you. Let our exultation be:

We are reborn. Praise God.

Going Home

World-weary and travel-worn, we turned our dusty black sedan down the long gravel driveway. At the end ahead of us, waiting, was an old, Swiss-style house, all peaks and doors and sweeping curves and decks. Parking on the slab of concrete, we turned off the car and climbed into the dusky air. One of the two French double doors opened before us, and a small head poked out.

"Mommy! Daddy!" she exclaimed.

We were home.

...

Is home where the heart is? Is it a place that completes us? Is it people who own a part of us? Is it a state of being? What makes home *home*, and how do we know when we're not there anymore?

One way or another, at the start of December Sarah and I left home and set out on our adventure. We had been commuting daily up to Seattle for medical appointments, but we had reached the point in my treatment path where that was no longer an option. When we left home, though, we weren't just leaving a structure or what was familiar: I was going to be spending quite an extended period in the hospital, so we had to leave our two daughters behind as well.

It might sound like an incredible break to leave the children behind and have a long-term "second honeymoon." (Though, admittedly, the setting does lack a certain ambiance no matter who you are.) Let me assure you, it's not. Especially as Christmas came and went and then New Years passed by as well, the conspicuous absence of our girls gnawed at us.

Things got better after the stint in the hospital. Then we were living in a little apartment minutes away from the clinic, but at least we weren't still trapped in the one tiny room. Nevertheless, we still found ourselves to be strangers in a foreign land.

In most of the great triumphant stories the heroes come back from their adventures wiser, stronger, with all they've learned and seen and experienced packed down inside. And there they stay, until the next odyssey comes along. Alternatively, the people who have become their home enfold them, and though the location is different, they come home all the same.

We thrill in the adventure, but eventually, even if it is bittersweet, we want the heroes to get home, whatever that home may be. Why? Because we want the heroes to live happily ever after, at least until the next adventure.

Why do we so love these stories? Why do we revel in these other lives? I think it's because, deep inside, we long for these heroes to be us. What we don't realize is, *they are*.

Maybe you don't see the adventure in your life. Maybe you don't see the importance of your quest. But that's because you don't see the full story. You don't fathom your own significance. And you don't realize the deep-seated hope that some day you'll be home.

So what if you're already home? What of this restlessness you feel in your heart? What about the feeling that you're supposed to do something important, and it's pushing and filling you almost to bursting?

I think this deserves a three-pronged answer. First of all, sometimes we seek adventure, not realizing that our adventure is all around us, right where we're at. Second of all, sometimes there is something we are pressing toward and we don't even completely realize what we're fighting for. But when it arrives, when we break through to the other side, we will sigh with relief, knowing this was what we were meant to find all along. Third of all, there is another home we are traveling to. And we are not there yet.

"These all died in faith, not having received the things promised, but having seen them and greeted them from afar, and having acknowledged that they were strangers and exiles on the earth. For people who speak thus make it clear that they are seeking a homeland. If they had been thinking of that land from which they had gone out, they would have had opportunity to return. But as it is, they desire a better country, that is, a heavenly one. Therefore God is not ashamed to be called their God, for he has prepared for them a city."[55]

How can we be home and yet so far from it? Because we are not *at* our true home yet. Yes, home is people. Yes, home is a place. And anything we have now is but a shadow of the people and place that is to come. And the adventure is to get there, to that true home. Not that the adventure ends there, of course: in fact, when we come home is when the adventure really begins.

"And as He spoke He no longer looked to them like a lion; but the things that began to happen after that were so great and beautiful that I cannot write them. And for us this is the end of all the stories, and we can most truly say that they all lived happily ever after. But for them it was only the beginning of the real story. All their life in this world and all their adventures in Narnia had only been the cover and the title page: now at last they were beginning Chapter One of the Great Story which no one on earth has read: which goes on forever: in which every chapter is better than the one before."[56]

We were homesick for our place and people in this world. But all of us are homesick for another home as well. And some day we will arrive there.

Having said all that, we must all have those rests, those "happily ever afters" in-between. No matter how brief. And it is so wonderful to say that, after our travels in foreign lands, we again found ourselves coming home.

Next week we start on another adventure, once again stepping out into the unknown. But for now we are home, and we are living our happily ever after. And that is a good feeling.

A Wonderful World

Sometimes it's easy to forget how beautiful the world around us is.

In fact, many of us have.

We are often so consumed with hate one for another, or fear for the future, or stress about work and family and life. We are so overwhelmed with the tragic, grungy particulars screaming for our attention that we completely miss the gorgeous, quiet elephant in the middle of the room.

How is it that amidst all the bright sparks one dark incident can ruin a day? How is it that one heated conversation can burn a whole week? Or a whole friendship?

We drive down the road, and as we go the traffic grinds to a dead halt. Twenty minutes later we see why we have been driving so intolerably slowly: there was a car accident, and everyone stopped to look at it. We are drawn to the tragic and the outrageous and the macabre. It's like we crave it. And I'm not talking about horror movies or "The Walking Dead:" I'm talking about the nightly news. I'm talking about talk radio. I'm talking about what's trending on Facebook and Twitter. I'm talking about car accidents on the freeway.

It can be so easy to be consumed by the latest horrible headline. To be overwhelmed by the evils men do, whether to the earth or to each other. To completely miss the fabulous, awesome truth.

We live in a wonderful world.

When God created the universe with a singular, exultant bang, when He split the light and matter and fashioned stars and supernovae and spun out galaxies, He said that it was good. When He finally created a rocky planet and filled it with water and dry land and life, He said that it was good. When He created us, He said that we were good.

That is as true today as it was all those many years ago.

Has evil insinuated and corrupted and ravaged? Yes. Absolutely. But that doesn't have to be what we *see*. We can choose to see something else. We can choose to see something greater, deeper and truer. And furthermore, we can help that Best to conquer.

In the Lord's prayer, Jesus says that we should pray "Your

kingdom come, your will be done, on earth as it is in heaven."[57] So why are we always praying to leave this world when God wants His goodness, His love and His light to shine here on earth? After all, what is His kingdom but utter paradise? And He wants that paradise to blaze where all will see it. One could call it a city on a hill, if one wanted to.[58]

Why spend so much time decrying the world when we can spend that time fighting and working and praying to make it better? We aren't wasting our energy polishing the brass on a sinking ship:[59] we are calling this world good along with its Creator. We are flaunting God's righteousness in the face of evil, and declaring that hate and corruption and vileness will not win the day. All it takes for evil to triumph is for good men to stand by and do nothing.[60]

There is hope in this good creation. There are glimmers of Heaven all around us, and we can see it every day if we look. But first we need to change our perspective. And we need to see the good.

"Why are you cast down, O my soul,
and why are you in turmoil within me?
Hope in God; for I shall again praise him,
my salvation and my God."[61]

"I give thanks to my Creator for this wonderful life where each of us has the opportunity to learn lessons we could not fully comprehend by any other means."
  - *Joseph B. Wirthlin*[62]

"We live in a wonderful world that is full of beauty, charm and adventure. There is no end to the adventures that we can have if only we seek them with our eyes open."
  - *Jawaharlal Nehru*[63]

"And I think to myself,
What a wonderful world."
 - *Louis Armstrong*[64]

Afterword

We live in uncertain times. Just like we always have, and always will. As Benjamin Franklin's adage so succinctly puts it, "In this world nothing can be said to be certain, except death and taxes." But it is in this truth that arises the possibility of great adventure.

After all, if everything were a sure bet, where would the fun be? We'd be alive, but could you really call it life?

There is the possibility of cancer. But there is also the possibility of influencing and helping people who you never would have met otherwise. There is the chance of great discomfort. But there is also the chance of incredible miracles *amidst* that discomfort. There can descend a darkness over your whole world. But there can also rise a wondrous light to guide you through.

Cancer changed my life. Was it hard? Absolutely. But it gave me the jolt I needed to get me moving, and the jolt many others needed as well. I shudder to think what my life would now be like without the year 2014. I suspect it would be much more of the "same old, same old." And the "same old, same old" was killing me all on its own.

Does it seem strange to hear me talking about getting

cancer in this way? Almost like it was a good thing? Yeah, I suppose it is. But it's moments like this that define our lives. We can use them to change us for the better, or we can allow them to impact us for the worse.

A lot of the time we try to isolate ourselves from the strange, scary world that throbs and beats and creeps around us. We insulate ourselves in our comfortably familiar setting and stay in our safe little bubble, believing that the bad is *out there,* and it could never get *in here.* And in so doing we slowly, imperceptibly, succumb to what Rob Bell calls "death by wallpaper and flooring."[65]

The adventure is there. The healing is there. The wonder is there. And often they are hidden just under the surface of our greatest struggles. Suffering can be a blessing in disguise. And it is usually in suffering that we find our greatest stories.

The last time I wrote an afterword for a book, I said I had rarely been so unmoored in my life. But sometimes we have to let ourselves become unmoored so that we can see where God wants to guide our little boat. In "Where We Go From Here" I mentioned the story of Hananiah, Mishael and Azariah. I went in the blazing furnace. And inside I met that fourth man who preserved me and brought me through. And I know He will be there for every furnace as the years draw on.

But that's my story. What's yours? Yours is in there, I know it. Maybe you're in the middle of living it right now, or maybe it happened ten years ago. Whatever the case, it's time to look at it from a different angle. It's time to see it not as the great negative, but as the little positives that changed you, taught you, and shaped the person you are today. And then it's time to tell that story. There are people who need to hear it. *I* need to hear it. Don't discount what you have to offer. You won't believe how your history will change another person's present.

As for me, there will be other books, but "The Cancer Diaries" are done. Even if cancer should come back at some point, I don't know that I'd have enough to add to make it worthwhile. I suppose we'll see. But, if you've enjoyed this book, definitely keep your eyes peeled for more.

Speaking of which, if you *have* been impacted by this book, would you do me a favor? Share it with someone who needs it. Give it to someone who would enjoy it. Review it on Amazon. Spread the word. I won't get this message out without your help. *You* will make it soar.

Thank you for reading. I hope it's showed you a new way of looking at the world. I hope it's helped reveal the wonder all around us. And I hope it's given you a fresh glimpse of God.

God bless you, my friend. Until next time.

(Did I succeed? =)[66]

Your Friend,

Byron Leavitt

Byron Leavitt
October, 2015
byron@byronleavitt.com

Appendixes and More

10 Things to Do if You Get Cancer
Appendix One

There are very few sentences as terrifying as the phrase, "You have cancer." If you've read any of this book you know that I understand exactly where you're at right now, whether it's a recurrence or the first time. This is one of the most confusing, shocking, numbing, overwhelming experiences you are likely to go through. And on top of everything else, there are so many voices out there telling you what to do and how to do it and why this is happening. Not to add another sound to the cacophony, but I just wanted to pass on a few things that got me through.

As you read this, though, please remember: **I am not a doctor.** This is not medical advice. This is just me doing what I can to help you. With that in mind, I also sincerely doubt that these steps are at all limited to just dealing with cancer. That's just what *I* went through. But if you're fighting something else, still give this a read. You never know what will give you the boost you need to make it.

Okay. Without further ado, here we go.

1. Resolve that you are going to make it. This might sound simplistic, weird or presumptuous, but I can attest that it is one of the most important things on this list. Why? Because "attitude determines altitude."[67] To put it another way: the people who think they are going to die, do. I've seen it happen over and over. When a person finally resolves that they aren't going to make it, they're right. Now, does this guarantee you'll live? No. But it boosts your chances considerably. I have read several articles stating this as well as had multiple medical professionals claim it, but all I can really say is: it worked for me. When they tell you there is a 30% chance you'll beat the cancer, that means that 30% of the people before you did. *Why not you?* No matter how difficult things get, *resolve that you will live.*

2. Bring others with you. Set in your mind that you're not just fighting for you. You're in it for others. And not only your family, or your friends (though you're certainly battling for them, too): you are in this to help the people who are hurting right next to you. An amazing thing happens when you decide to do this: *it takes the focus off of you.* This makes all of your problems just that little bit smaller, and the smaller they get, the easier they are to handle. It also makes your vision that much greater. You will realize just what you have to offer, even in (or perhaps because of) your broken state, to the scared, wounded people around you.

3. Turn the conversation. You will encounter many people who just won't know how to talk to you any more. They will stutter something like, "I'm so sorry to hear about what you're going through." Or, very quietly, "How are you *doing?*" They might follow that up with, "Cancer killed my cousin/mother/friend/acquaintance." First of all, their pain is real. And they don't know how to handle it. Having said that, you can't keep that negativity around you. So, you have two options: throw the baby out with the bathwater and tell this person you can't be around them because of their negative outlook, or turn the conversation. Of course, for this to work you actually have to *be* in a good place yourself, and have decided you are going to do steps one and two above. But if you are and you have, tell them, "You know, I'm actually not doing that bad." Or, "Yeah, it's hard, but I'm going to get through it." If you're a Christian, use faith. (This is when this really works.) Say, "God's been with me all the way." Or, "You wouldn't believe some of the miracles I've seen." Or something similar. This will automatically flip the conversation from negative to positive. The person (who is looking to *you* for pointers on how to interact with you now) will adopt your attitude, and suddenly a funeral dirge will become a triumphant exultation. This helps you, and it also helps them.

4. Stop asking why. "Why me?" "But I'm a good person." "What did I do to deserve this?" "Why is this happening?" "How did I get here?" "Am I being punished?" "I've always been so healthy." "Did I eat something wrong?" "Is this all a test?" "Was it in my genes?" "Does God hate me?" It is so easy to rip yourself apart with the question (and its offshoots,) "Why me?" Now, sure, perhaps an honest reflection or two can be advantageous. For instance, "Oh, maybe I got this cancer because I've been smoking like a chimney for fifteen years" can help lead you to some positive change. But asking over and over "Why me?" or one of its various offspring will cause you nothing but anguish. You will hear many, many theories as to why it happened. But the truth is this: *you will likely never know why*. So don't shred yourself into ribbons over a question that has no answer. You're already here. There's nothing you can change about what was. It's time to fight.

5. Cling to the stubborn optimists. (Starting to see a trend in this list yet?) Realism and caution are good in many situations. You need doses of both to prepare you for every eventuality down many of life's paths. But if "realism" is really just fear and pessimism under a different title, it will work with cancer to kill you. Sometimes, though, it's hard to be up. At those times find the stubborn optimists, the ones who say you'll make it no matter what, and cling to them. No matter how rose-tinted the glasses, these are the champions who will fight tooth-and-nail to see you survive. They are your best advocates. They are your best friends. Embrace them.

6. Choose prayer. Don't underestimate the power of prayer. Not a Christian? Fine. Then find Christians to pray for you. But I highly encourage you to embrace it yourself, in addition to getting others to pray for you. Prayer opens you up, and it opens the world around you up. I have seen too many difficulties resolved and too much miraculous happenstance to ever rule out prayer. Having said that, is all prayer created equal? Definitely not. If someone is praying for you to get well "if it be God's will," they aren't doing you too many favors. If they're praying for you to get through this "after your time in the fire has ended," that's not great either. You want people who will *go to war* for you. People who will say, "Oh God, heal her!" Can't find those people? Give me a ring. You'll find the contact info in a couple of pages. If you're still unsure about this whole prayer thing, not a problem. It's a free country. But let me pose a question to you: *what can it possibly hurt?* And, furthermore, what if *it really does help?*

7. Roll with the punches. This one might seem self-evident, but I'm going to mention it anyway. During your time fighting cancer it might feel like you're walking a tightrope over a pit of razer blades. And, sometimes, you will get cut. Whether it's a questionable CAT scan or a really bad chemo or the news that the cancer has returned, there are plenty of opportunities to bleed while fighting this monster. But don't let the cuts take you down. Bandage yourself up, and get back in the fight. Say you just learned the cancer has come back. Fine. Then it's going to be a piece of cake to whoop it a second (or third) time.

8. Don't be afraid to accept help. If you're anything like me, the thought of someone doing something sizable for you might just roil your guts. But here's the truth: this process is going to take a lot out of you, and it's going to require a ton of time, energy and willpower. You won't be able to make it alone. *You need help.* If someone offers to mow your lawn, let them. If someone wants to donate money to you, let them. It will take pressure off of you, and it will make them feel like they're making a difference. For me this is a hard and bitter pill to swallow. Maybe it's not for you. But whether it is or isn't, it's a pill you need to swallow, regardless.

9. Take a deep breath. Every once in a while you will find yourself winding tighter and tighter and tighter, and eventually you'll realize you're about to snap. You just can't take it any more. When this happens, take a deep breath. Check out from the world for a little bit. Get your bearings. Do what you need to do to get back into a good place where you can move forward. *You're going to be okay. You're going to make it.* Don't let these dark spots mask the light at the end of the tunnel.

10. Embrace God. If you've read any of this book, this one shouldn't surprise you. (In fact, none of these probably have.) But I don't think I would have survived if I hadn't relied so heavily on God. This is something that will perhaps be easier for me than for you, because I have spent a lifetime building a relationship with God. But whether you've been a devoted Christian since birth or you're an agnostic just starting to think there might be Something there after all, I think there is great comfort, wisdom and strength in making God a part of your journey. But what does that mean, exactly, to rely on God? And how do you do it? You must start by knowing who God is. Both near-death experiences and the Bible tell us that, at His core, God is an overwhelming, overpowering force of pure love. So start from the place of assuming that God is with you, and that He is, in fact, *suffering* with you. That, indeed, He has you cradled in the palm of His hand, and that no matter how bad things get you have a good Father who cares deeply for you. Then know that He has a plan to turn all things to good for those that love Him. That, no matter how this goes, there is a good outcome for you. Even if you should lose this battle with cancer, know that what comes next will be so much better than this present suffering.

No matter what circumstance brings, your future is bright. You can survive this; you can make it through. I'm here for you, too, and if there's anything I can do for you don't hesitate to let me know.

Need Prayer?
Appendix Two

If you're currently battling cancer or you know someone who is, I want to help. Or maybe it's some other furnace you find yourself in. I want to help with that, too.

On my website, lifespringseternal.com, I have a prayer list devoted strictly to people going through cancer or other very serious conditions. If you would like to be added to this list, contact me at byron@byronleavitt.com. I would love to talk with you, and I would love to get others praying for you.

You don't have to go through this alone. There's a whole slew of people who would love to stand with you. I don't want anything from you, and you've got nothing to lose. Why not send me a note today?

Life Springs

Life Springs is a place of wonder, darkness and hope. It is also the place where I post all my newest and freshest thoughts, ponderings, rantings, etc. If you've enjoyed this book, then you'd enjoy Life Springs. You should check it out at http://www.lifespringseternal.com.

While you're there, sign up for the e-mail list to become a part of the Life Springs family!

What Did You Think?

No matter what your take on this book, I would greatly appreciate a review on Amazon, Kindle, Good Reads, Nook or your platform of choice! I'd love to hear what you think!

I would also love to hear from you personally. Drop me a line when you have a minute at byron@byronleavitt.com. Or meet me either on Facebook at http://www.facebook.com/byroncleavitt or on Twitter at http://www.twitter.com/byron_leavitt. God bless you.

References

Dare to Hope

1. Job 13:15

2. Psalms 20:7-8

Beauty in the Rain

3. Daniel 3

4. Image © IStock Photo

Coauthoring Our Destinies

5. Gen. 18:22-33

6. Gen. 4:10

7. Jonah 1:2

There is Peace

8. Matthew 8:23-27; Luke 8:22-25

9. Simon Wiesenthal, "The Sunflower: On the Possibilities and Limits of Forgiveness" (Schocken, 1998).

10. Philippians 4:7

This Island, Man

11. Robert Zemeckis, "Castaway" (Twentieth Century Fox Film Corporation, 2000).

12. Rob Bell, "Drops Like Stars" (Zondervan, 2009).

Our Healer

13. Michael Guglielmucci, "Healer" (Integrity Media, 2008).

14. Mark Batterson, "The Circle Maker" (Zondervan, 2011).

15. Kings 20:1-7

16. Peter 2:24

Life Springs Eternal

17. Psalms 6:5; Psalms 18:5; for more on Sheol, check out the Wikipedia page at http://en.wikipedia.org/wiki/Sheol

18. Ecclesiastes 3:21

19. Ecclesiastes 9:5

20. John 5:29; 1 Corinthians 15:12-21

21. Matthew 22:23; Mark 12:18; Luke 20:27; Acts 23:8; for more on the Sadducees and Pharisees, check out: http://www.catholic.com/quickquestions/please-explain-the-difference-between-the-sadducees-and-the-pharisees-in-the-gospels

22. Randy Alcorn, "Heaven" (Tyndale House Publishers, 2004), 475-482. For more on the Platonic influence

on Christianity, check out: http://geekychristian.com/christianitys-platonic-heaven/

23. Jeffrey Long & Paul Perry, "Evidence of the Afterlife" (HarperOne, 2010). Howard Storm, "My Descent into Death" (Doubleday, 2005). Richard Sigmund, "My Time in Heaven" (Whitaker House, 2010). Mary C. Neal, MD, "To Heaven and Back" (Water Brook Press, 2012). For more on Near Death Experiences, check out http://www.nderf.org.

24. For a thorough examination of the biblical references to Heaven, see Randy Alcorn's book of the same name. (Randy Alcorn, "Heaven" (Tyndale House Publishers, 2004).) I also recommend Dinesh D'Souza's book on the afterlife. (Dinesh D'Souza, "Life After Death: The Evidence" (Regnery Publishing, 2009).)

25. Luke 23:43

26. Corinthians 12:2-3

27. Samuel Stennett, "On Jordan's Stormy Banks I Stand" (1787).

28. 1 Corinthians 15:55b

Where We Go From Here

29. Proverbs 13:12

30. 2 Corinthians 4:1, 6-10, 16-18

Joy in the Holding

31. John 15:11

32. John 16:22

33. Romans 14:17

34. Romans 15:13

35. James 1:2-4

A Violent Love

36. Deuteronomy 4:24

37. Matthew 11:12

Behind Our Masks

38. 1 Corinthians 9:19-23

Prayer Like Summer Rain

39. Matthew 6:9-13

40. Psalm 23

41. Luke 10:19; Mark 16:14-18

Embracing the Mystery

42. https://en.wikipedia.org/wiki/Thirty_Years%27_War

43. 1 Peter 3:21

44. 2. Acts 10:44-48

45. http://www.reasons.org

46. Isaiah 55:8-9

47. Psalms 145:3

In the Bleak Mid-Winter

48. Christina Rosetti, "In the Bleak Midwinter" (1872). Includes additional lyrics by Jars of Clay (Nettwerk Records, 2007).

I Heard the Bells

49. Henry Wadsworth Longfellow, "Christmas Bells" (1863).

Holy Ghost

50. Ecclesiastes 1:2

51. Here's evangelist Charles Finney's story of meeting the Holy Ghost: http://www.lit4ever.org/baptism.html – Here's revivalist Evan Robert's experience: http://www.revivaltimes.org/index.php?aid=803 – Here's the founder of the Methodist Church, John Wesley's story – http://www.christianitytoday.com/ch/131christians/denominationalfounders/wesley.html?start=1

In Our Ruins

52. Ruth 1-4

The Seattle Journal Part 5

53. https://www.goodreads.com/quotes/987-there-are-only-two-ways-to-live-your-life-one

We Are Reborn

54. John 3:1-21

Going Home

55. Hebrews 11:13-16

56. C.S. Lewis, "The Last Battle" (HarperCollins, 1994).

A Wonderful World

57. Matthew 6:10

58. Matthew 5:14

59. Quote by J. Vernon McGee

60. Paraphrased from a quote by Edmund Burke

61. Psalms 42:11

62. http://www.brainyquote.com/quotes/keywords/wonderful_life.html#FBy1Tmzv4u3M5M31.99

63. http://www.searchquotes.com/search/Wonderful_World/

64. Bob Thiele & George David Weiss, "What a Wonderful World" (First recorded by Louis Armstrong; "What a Wonderful World", ABC 10982, HMV; 1967).

Afterword

65. Rob Bell, "Drops Like Stars" (Zondervan, 2009).

66. Don't remember this? See page 7.

Appendix: 10 Things to Do if You Get Cancer

67. This is a paraphrase of a Zig Ziglar quote. View the full quote at http://www.brainyquote.com/quotes/quotes/z/zigziglar381975.html.

Topical Index

Acceptance

    Cross-Stitched Lives   42

    This Island, Man   46

    Embracing the Mystery   103

Beauty

    Beauty in the Rain   26

    A Wonderful World   161

Beliefs

    Prayer Like Summer Rain   93

    Why Do You Believe That?   98

    Embracing the Mystery   103

Bleakness

    Dare to Hope   22

    Where We Go From Here   62

Advent: I Heard the Bells	118
Advent	122
Holy Ghost	132
In Our Ruins	136

Christmas

Advent: In the Bleak Mid-Winter	114
Advent: I Heard the Bells	118
Advent	122

Courage

Beauty in the Rain	26
Where We Go From Here	62

Death

Life Springs Eternal	58
In Our Ruins	136
We are Reborn	151

Despair

Where We Go From Here	62

Destiny

Coauthoring Our Destinies	29

Forgiveness

Cross-Stitched Lives	42

Healing

    Our Healer   54

Hope

    Dare to Hope   22

Identity

    Behind Our Masks   84

Joy

    Joy in the Holding   76

Love

    Wondering and Grateful   14

    A Violent Love   80

    Advent   122

Panic

    Dare to Hope   22

    There is Peace   39

    The Art of Human Being   141

Peace

    There is Peace   39

Prayer

    Our Healer   54

    Prayer Like Summer Rain   93

Suffering

Wondering and Grateful	14
Beauty in the Rain	26
Joy in the Holding	76
We are Reborn	151

Story

Coauthoring Our Destinies	29
Going Home	156

Rest

The Art of Human Being	141

Wonder

Wondering and Grateful	14
Beauty in the Rain	26
Life Springs Eternal	58
Advent: In the Bleak Midwinter	114
Advent: I Heard the Bells	118
Advent	122
Holy Ghost	132
In Our Ruins	136
We are Reborn	151
Going Home	156
A Wonderful World	161

Acknowledgments

Book One

I always read that it takes a lot of people to write a book.

I don't know about that. I did pretty much this whole thing by myself. The only help I really got was from my wife and a couple semi-critical eyes, as well as some InDesign training videos.

However, I do believe it takes a lot of people to live a life. Especially when you've been living one like I have this past year.

First, thanks to my mother-in-law, Pam, who moved in with us while I was flat on my back and Sarah had her broken toe. We wouldn't have made it through without her. And thanks to my father-in-law, Michael, for giving her up for those months.

Second, thanks to my aunt, Julie, who drove up from Oregon repeatedly to help us and to accompany us to appointments as well as bringing us supplies, remedies, medicine and solutions. She went above and beyond.

Thanks are due also to Mandy, my coworker, who went all kinds of crazy guard dog at work. From putting in air purifiers to hanging up signs that ours was a germ-free office to telling everyone -- including our boss -- that, no, I couldn't be talked to right then no matter how urgent it seemed, she was (and is) awesome.

Thanks to my dad, Chris, and new mom, Marilyn, for always being willing to free up their schedules. Thanks to Peter for understanding my early frustrations with "Invalid Byron." Thanks to Bob and Marissa for dropping everything to drive over monthly from Spokane. Thanks to my mom, Val, my sister, Dawn, and my brothers-in-law Jared and Andrew for their support. Thanks to Pastor Dwain, Pastor Joel, Michael, Harold and the whole office staff for putting up with my absences for doctor's appointments and the occasional weekend, as well as for the prayers.

Speaking of which, thank you to every single person, whether I know you or not, who prayed for me. Your prayers were felt. Your prayers were answered. And they will be again.

Thanks to Eileen, Lauri, Patsy, Dereck, Jack, Barbara, Pastor Gayle and the New Life gang, Kathleen, Teresa and Rick, Steve and Eric. You know what you did (well, at least you probably know what you did.) And it was life-changing.

Thanks to Dr. Chaves, Amy, Debbie, Rita, Deb and the rest of the Northwest Medical Specialties staff. You are all remarkable human beings, and ministering angels for God whether you believe in Him or not. Thanks to all of the chemo patients, too, who let us into their lives - if only for a few hours. May you find healing in the arms of the Healer. (Here's looking at you, Herb and Beth.)

Thanks to everyone who gave to us financially. I honestly don't even know who all of you were. But *you* do. And I thank you.

Thanks to everyone who gave me encouragement on the blog and let me know how much it was meaning to them. You kept me going. This book wouldn't exist without you.

Thanks to everyone I forgot to mention. Your contribution changed our lives, and just because my memory sucks doesn't mean you aren't valued and cherished.

Almost last but definitely not least, thank you to the most important people in my life, the ones without whom I wouldn't have beaten cancer (or had any reason to): my wife, Sarah (my butterfly), my daughter, Aurora (my princess), my daughter, Eden (my pipsqueak), and my savior, Jesus Christ (my brother and my Lord). I love you all. Once more for the win.

Thank you, God. Your mercies endure forever.

Book Two

Just as with the first book, I am amazed at how many people it took to get us through the second half of the year. It was a singularly singular experience (as in me, Sarah, and, um...), but at the same time there was a whole army standing behind us. With that in mind, if I miss you it's due to poor memory or lack of knowledge and not that you and your contribution aren't cherished.

First, thanks to Pam and Michael Adams, Sarah's parents, for taking care of Aurora and Eden.

Thanks to Dawn and Jared Postlethwaite for also taking care of the girls. And for Christmas.

Thanks to my dad, Chris Leavitt, and new mom, Marilyn,

for being such amazing support mentally, physically and financially. And for telling everyone about my book. =)

Thanks to Andy and Anna Murphy. You guys are incredible. We should hang out more.

Next, thanks to Peter Adams. You, sir, are a gentleman of singular vision, taste, and demeanor, a scholar of the highest musical repute, and a stellar human being to boot.

Thanks to Rick and Teresa Wheeler, Barbara Roper, and Mary Farnsworth for their unflagging support through cards.

Thanks to Sue, Terry and Margie Murphy for all of their help, whether in rallying troops, financially, or prayerfully.

Thanks to Dale, Sally and the whole McCarty family, Dana Pittman, Steve and Tyler Olels, and Eileen Larsen for their amazing financial support. Thanks to Steve and Jann Barclift, as well as Tom and Joletta Holman. Thanks also to World Outreach Ministries Foundation for feeling our cause a worthy one.

Speaking of financial support, an enormous thank you to everyone who gave to us financially through New Horizon, one of the fundraisers, or through some other avenue. I don't know who you are, and I'm sorry I can't mention your name here. But *you* know who you are, and you know what you did. You got us through. *Thank you.*

Thanks to Kathleen Thomas for tirelessly running the Caring Bridge site and fundraisers, even though I never supplied her with any information. (Seriously. I don't think Kathleen could have had a worse person to be helping in that way.)

Thanks to those who visited us when we were most down:

Jarid and Melinda Maker, Mandy Kaplan and Jason Treadwell, Jon and Iana Frederickson, and Lyle and Haeran Smith. Thanks to Colleen for opening her home.

Thanks to our family, Valerie Leavitt, Josh and Angela Adams, Andrew Adams, Julie Ackelson, and Robert and Marissa Leavitt, for their support through finances, visiting, and prayer.

Thanks to the teams at Seattle Cancer Care Alliance, the University of Washington, and Northwest Medical Specialties. I'm alive because of you.

Many, many thanks to everyone who prayed for us, and also to those who committed (and are still committing) to the prayer list. You made, and continue to make, miracles happen. Keep it up!

Thanks to everyone who let me know how much the blog was meaning to them, and who shared it with their friends. I appreciated the comments, and I appreciate you.

Much love to my daughters Aurora and Eden, who grew up so much mentally, emotionally and spiritually during this time.

More love and even more thanks to my wife, Sarah, who rabidly latched on and wouldn't let go through this entire process. You only ever left when I forced you to, and you endured so much for me. May your sacrifice never be understated or undervalued. I love you, butterfly.

Thank you, God. Thank you, Jesus. Thank you, Holy Spirit. Your incredible, uncontainable love surprises me anew every day. I never get tired of seeing your miracles, and of seeing lives changed for your glory.

About Byron

Byron Leavitt lives near Tacoma, Washington in a centennial Swiss-style home surrounded by carnivorous plants and Morning Glory. He is joined by the love of his life, Sarah, their daughters Aurora and Eden, their stoic butler, Egad, and their gremlin, Brain. Occasionally people have commented negatively about the dragons, the gargoyle baby, the basement, Harvey, or even about Egad himself. Such comments always make Byron smile.

Byron is the author of "The Cancer Diaries", as well as the forthcoming novel "The Fish in Jonah's Puddle (To Say Nothing of the Demon)", which you can read chapter by chapter as he writes it on Life Springs (http://www.lifespringseternal.com.) You can learn more about his work on his website, http://www.byronleavitt.com.

When he is not writing in the third person, Byron will often address you as himself. Hi.

The Fish in Jonah's Puddle

Jonah is a boy with an overactive imagination. Or is he?

What if there really is a troll in his basement, a harpy in the trees and a salmon swimming in a puddle behind his house? What if some of the puddles from the last rainstorm really *did* lead to other dimensions? And what if his parents really *had* just accidentally stepped into the belly of a demon?

Welcome to "The Fish in Jonah's Puddle (To Say Nothing of the Demon)". It's a book unlike anything you've read before. And you can read it for free, chapter by chapter, as I release it on Life Springs.

Just go to http://www.lifespringseternal.com to start reading today!

Join the Conversation.

http://www.LifeSpringsEternal.com

http://www.facebook.com/ByronCLeavitt

http://www.twitter.com/Byron_Leavitt

http://www.ByronLeavitt.com

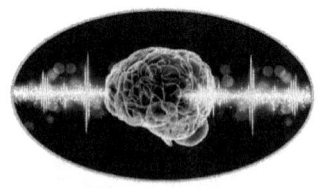

Brain Waves Press

www.ingramcontent.com/pod-product-compliance
Lightning Source LLC
Chambersburg PA
CBHW070147100426
42743CB00013B/2844